ETHICAL DECISIONS FOR SOCIAL WORK PRACTICE

ll0669092

To Chaya and Sylvia

ETHICAL DECISIONS
FOR SOCIAL WORK PRACTICE

Frank Loewenberg · Ralph Dolgoff
Bar-Ilan University   **Adelphi University**

F.E. PEACOCK PUBLISHERS, INC.
ITASCA, ILLINOIS 60143

Copyright © 1982
F. E. Peacock Publishers, Inc.
All rights reserved
Library of Congress
Catalog Card Number 81-82888
ISBN #0-87581-273-2
Printed in the U.S.A.

Table of Contents

Table of Exemplars of Ethical Dilemmas and Decisions

Preface

In the contemporary world, professionals are increasingly under pressure to deal with difficult ethical problems. In social work, students encounter such problems early in field instruction as they learn to work in highly complex human situations. Social work practitioners are confronted daily with dilemmas which demand clarity about professional values and ethics. In recent years, professional organizations, colleges, universities, and professional schools, recognizing the need, have given more attention to the area of ethics. With the adoption of a new code of ethics by the National Association of Social Workers, social work has also focused interest on professional ethics.

The growing power of consumerism in American life has forced all professions to reexamine their ethical stance. And it may be, as one professor was heard to say at a recent social work conference, that "In the 1970s social workers were charged with being ineffective, in the 1980s they will be charged with being immoral." These and other factors give greater urgency to the need to face the many ethical problems and dilemmas with which social workers wrestle almost daily.

In this book we will not present prescriptions or rules which can be applied blindly under any and all circumstances. Instead the thrust will be on helping social work students and practitioners to learn to analyze the ethical problems and issues which they will and do face in the field. To help them in this test we have presented some of the philosophical and theoretical background material. But our focus throughout will be on social work practice and social work practitioners, in order to help the reader think through the ethical problems and dilemmas which occur in social work practice.

This focus on the individual—individual client as well as individual worker—is congruent with the emphasis which American society has given to the individual. Yet we recognize that the individual, though important, is not everything. There certainly is need to go beyond the individual dilemma and to consider ethical issues in professional, societal, and communal terms. At the same time, most contemporary social workers (and not only clinical social workers in private practice) work with individuals, families, or small groups. Even social workers in community work and community development generally practice with individuals, and their concern is directed toward the effect of the environment on individuals and families.

Our focus on the individual is not meant to indicate a preference for psychotherapy or the medical model of intervention, nor does it deny one of the basic assumptions of contemporary social work practice—that problems arise at the interface of the person and environment. Instead, this focus simply recognizes the reality that most social work practice is with individuals, families, and small groups and not with macrosystems and large scale societies.

The case examples in this book are real but none occurred in the way they are described or to the people identified in each situation. Neither first nor second names nor identifying information came from social agency records or social workers. Needless to say the case examples do not always typify good or desirable practice but were chosen to illustrate ethical practice problems.

We want to thank all of our colleagues and students at Adelphi University School of Social Work and at the University of Pennsylvania School of Social Work for helping us think through the issues involved in social work ethics. We are especially thankful to Kay Dea, Arthur Eaton, Gertrude Goldberg, Malvina Gordon, Robert Mason, Catherine Papell, Beulah Rothman, Eleanor Ryder, Brad Sheafor, Dean Louise Shoemaker, Joseph Soffen, and Dean Joseph Vigilante. We wish to thank our students and colleagues to whom we owe much, both teachers and practitioners, for the stimulation and help they have given us during the time that we prepared this book, but we alone are responsible for any errors of fact, judgment, or interpretation.

We want to express our appreciation to Sylvia Dolgoff, Karen Fine, Lucille Cambardella, and Solveig Sander who typed the manuscript.

Finally, our wives Chaya and Sylvia were active partners in developing this book and making it a readable one. We apologize to them and to our children who put up with part-time fathers and part-time husbands for far too long.

F.M.L.
R.D.

Garden City, New York
July 1980

1 Ethical Choices in Professional Life

The term *ethics* comes from the Greek root *ethos* which means custom, usage, or habit. But the subject of contemporary ethics goes far beyond mere custom or habit. It deals with the question of what is morally *right*. Professional ethics are concerned with the correct course of professional action. Social work ethics are designed to help social workers decide which of two or more goals or activities is the right one.

CONTEMPORARY INTEREST IN PROFESSIONAL ETHICS

Some may think it ironic that the interest in professional ethics has peaked just now, in the last third of a century which has not been characterized by a very high level of morality or by superior ethical conduct. This has been the century in which:

- more people have been killed by violence than in any previous century (and there are still two decades to go before the total number killed will be known);
- genocide was perfected by a nation considered by many to be one of the most cultured and most ethical, while all other nations stood by silently;
- the decrease of traditional authority, occurring simultaneously with the liberation of Blacks, women, gays, and others, has

1

accelerated what Nietzsche once called the "transvaluation of values";

- the tendency toward a pluralism of options has been extended to include a pluralism of ethics.

Rapid and extensive social change, along with technological development and innovation, has created many new problems. These same changes have also given social workers an opportunity to select relevant goals and strategies from a much greater number of options. Today's social workers face many more decisions than did social workers in earlier decades, yet societal criteria and guides are less clear than ever before. What can conscientious social workers do when they face complex ethical problems in a complicated world?

IS THERE A NEED FOR A CODE OF ETHICS?

The original NASW Code of Ethics as well as the revised NASW Code of Ethics (see Appendix B1), approved by the Delegate Assembly in 1979, are testimony to the fact that many social workers saw a need for such a guide. But questions about the usefulness of the revised code appeared even before it became an official document guiding the professional activities of all social workers: Don't social workers, like all intelligent people, know right from wrong instinctively? Do we really need a formal code of ethics to know that evil is evil? Will not any printed code of ethics be out of date in this rapidly changing society even before the ink is dry? Will not a code of ethics sometimes force social workers to do things they would rather not do? Is it possible for a code of ethical principles to be applicable for social work practice where no two situations are fully alike? And is it necessary to have ethical principles for professionals who are committed to practice in a nonjudgmental way?

These questions suggest the critical need to examine the place of professional ethics in social work practice. The bureaucratization of much of social work, as well as the increasing complexity of contemporary social structures, have tended to limit somewhat the scope of social workers' decisions. Nevertheless, modern social workers are faced almost continually by ethical problems which force them to make difficult choices.

WHAT ARE ETHICAL PROBLEMS IN SOCIAL WORK PRACTICE?

Ethical problems, like all practice problems, come in a great variety of forms. Here we will not develop an intricate typology, but instead we will present a number of examples of ethical problems faced by some social workers.

1.1: Planning Kevin's suicide

Kevin Gallagher, a sixteen-year-old high school student, has a spinal problem as a result of a sports injury suffered a few years ago. He has been receiving constant and painful treatments since the day he was injured.

Recently Kevin confided to his social worker that he had decided to commit suicide. The reason he wants to put an end to his life is that his widowed father wants to remarry and Kevin feels that he is in the way. His father also has business problems and finds it increasingly difficult to pay for his very expensive treatments. Kevin feels that he will die sooner or later anyhow. Why drag it out, he asked.

Kevin does not want anyone, not even his father, to know about his decision. He asked the social worker for help in finding a foolproof way to end his life.

- What ethical issues does this exemplar pose?
- How will the social worker decide what course of action to follow?
- Which ethical principles should guide the social worker in facing this ethical problem? Where will the social worker find these?

1.2:   Roy and Maureen White's future

Lillian and Harry White have been married for ten years,

but recently filed for divorce. During most of the ten years, theirs was a rather stormy marriage with many fights and a number of separations. Both have had numerous affairs. They have two children—five-year-old Maureen and three-year-old Roy. Harry has sued for divorce, charging that Lillian is a drug addict and, therefore, an unfit mother. Lillian has filed a countersuit, charging Harry with adultery and failure to support her and the children.

The court social worker has learned that both parents have been on heavy drugs. While Harry has good job prospects, he has been fired from his last six jobs (during the last two years) because of his inability to get along with fellow workers. Lillian moved away from Harry and her children a year ago in order to live with her lover, but returned three months later. As soon as the divorce is final she plans to share an apartment with her current lover. But she wants her children to be with her. Lillian has no employment skills and will require AFDC support.

Maureen and Roy are two bright and happy youngsters who seem to be unaware of their parents' stormy marital history. The social worker feels that the children are too young to be asked to choose the parent with whom they would prefer to live the next ten or fifteen years. But that is the problem facing the court.

- What ethical issues does this exemplar pose?
- How will the social worker decide what course of action to follow?
- Which ethical principles should guide the social worker in facing this ethical problem? Where will the social worker find these?

1.3: Don Andrew's threat

Don Andrew is the owner of a trucking firm and is a powerful person in Maryville politics. He enjoys a good reputation and is known as a warm father and an excellent husband. It came somewhat as a shock when the public health nurse informed the Child Protective Service that she suspected incestuous relations between Don Andrew and his twelve-year-old daughter Alice.

Russell Becker was assigned to investigate this report. Within a few days after the assignment, even before Becker had had a chance to become fully familiar with the details of the case, Don Andrew appeared one early evening at the Becker home. He said that he dropped by in order to help Becker. He had heard that some busybody nurse was spreading foolish stories about him and that, of course, there was no substance to what she said. He advised Becker to busy himself with other work and not bother the Andrew family which knew how to take care of itself without outside meddling. If Becker did not listen to him, he, Don Andrew, would make sure that Becker would be without a job. And Becker knew that Andrew had enough political power in Maryville to do just what he threatened to do.

- What ethical issue faces Russell Becker?
- How will Becker decide what to do?
- What ethical principles can guide Becker in reaching a decision?
- Where will he find these ethical principles?

ABOUT THIS BOOK

Some social workers will regret that this book does not present infallible moral guides, nor provide ready-made ethical answers. The reader will not be told what to do. Instead questions will be raised, possible consequences considered, and alternate options noted. The aim throughout is to alert the modern social worker to ethical issues and problems and to help practitioners become more capable in coping with these.

In Chapter 2 we will review the relation between values, general ethics, and professional ethics. We will examine the manifest and latent functions of professional ethics before presenting a brief history of the evolution of professional ethics in social work. Finally we will suggest that *freedom* and *power* are central issues in professional ethics and the cornerstone of most ethical problems.

In Chapter 3 we will discuss the basic ethical dilemmas facing social work practitioners. Through the use of exemplars the reader will be invited to examine each dilemma as it applies to and is derived from contemporary social work practice.

In Chapter 4 we will explicate the different phases of the ethical decision-making process as well as examine the various sources for social work ethics.

And in the fifth and last chapter we will present selected guides and ideas to help social workers implement and safeguard ethical decision-making in social work practice. Exercises will appear at the end of each chapter and additional exemplars can be found in the appendix.

Ethical problems will continue to cause discomfort even after you have read this book. This is so because every decision which a social worker makes entails ethical risks. Perhaps the most agonizing of these risks is the danger of making a choice which may hurt or damage a client. Yet these hazards are unavoidable and a social worker who cannot endure them, a social worker who cannot cope with the tensions which ethical problems create, will not be an effective practitioner. We hope that the discussions and questions raised in these pages will alert social workers to their ethical responsibilities and that, in this way, they will become better and more effective professionals.

EXERCISES

1. Describe an ethical problem which you have encountered in your practice or in your field work:
    a. What ethical issues are involved?
    b. Does the NASW Code of Ethics address itself to these issues? (See Appendix B1).
    c. List and analyze the options available for resolving this ethical problem.
2. Take any one of the exemplars from Appendix A and answer the questions posed for Exercise 1.

2 Professional Ethics in Social Work Practice

This book is addressed to social workers, not to philosophers. Yet any consideration of professional ethics must take into account the philosophic bases of ethics. Here we shall briefly define the terms *values* and *ethics*, attempt to identify the areas of concern of each, and explore the relationship of professional ethics to general societal ethics.

VALUES

Values is a word which is often used loosely. One popular dictionary offers no less than seventeen definitions for this term. Maslow (1962:158) observed that values can be thought of as a big container holding all sorts of miscellaneous and vague things. Most social scientists, however, have attempted to define the term more precisely. The most widely used definitions suggest that values are meant to serve as guides or criteria for selecting appropriate behaviors. Thus, Bartlett (1970:63) used the term value to refer to what is regarded as good and desirable. And Williams (1967:23) identified values as "those conceptions of desirable states of affairs that are utilized in selective conduct as criteria for preference or choice or as justifications for proposed or actual behavior."

Yet values often do not lead to the desired behaviors. Social workers, just as other professionals, are often painfully aware that their own practice activities seem to depart widely from societal values and even from professional values. Social workers, for example, value client participation in decision-making, yet do not always make an effort to fully involve their clients. One explanation for the lack of congruence between values and behaviors may be that values often occur at a high level of generality while behaviors are very specific. There is broad agreement about the most generalized values, such as cooperation and success, but these are not sufficiently specific to help in identifying appropriate behaviors. On the other hand, the more specific a value, the more useful it will be as a behavioral guide, but the smaller the chance that it will gain wide acceptance. For example, there is little disagreement in this society that "family life" is a highly desired value—little disagreement as long as this value is not defined in more specific operational terms. But this generalized value does not help an adult son who has to make difficult decisions about how to care for his paralyzed, bedridden father without increasing the tensions already existing between his present wife and the children from his previous marriage. Nor will the son's social worker find any specific ethical referents to provide guidance in this and similar situations. Recent national discussions about a national family policy also have revealed that various ethnic, religious, socioeconomic, and lifestyle groups hold many different specific values and perspectives around the generalized family-value to which almost all agree.

Just as there is wide agreement about generalized societal values, so is there a wide consensus about the basic value orientation of social work. Every professional social worker will agree that client participation, self-determination, and confidentiality are among the basic social work values. However, disagreements are likely to occur when these generalized social work values must be implemented. Social workers will differ about priorities, specific objectives, and the means necessary to implement these generalized values.

As long as basic professional values remain generalized and nonspecific, they do not offer behavioral guidance. Social workers are likely to engage in a variety of different, and sometimes even contradictory activities, even while claiming support from the same generalized values. This situation led Perlman (1976:381) to conclude that "a value has small worth, except as it is moved, or is moveable, from believing into doing, from verbal affirmation into action." Professional values which do not provide guidance and direction are of limited use for practitioners. But it has been suggested that ethical principles can be derived from these values and that these principles could serve as guides for practitioner behavior. When these principles are stated as professional ethics, they may provide social workers with criteria for making difficult practice decisions.

SOCIETAL ETHICS AND PROFESSIONAL ETHICS

Though the terms value and ethic are often used interchangeably, the two are not identical. Ethics are deduced from values and must be in consonance with them. The difference between them is that values are concerned with what is good and desirable, while ethics deal with what is right and correct. Every person's right to privacy, for example, is a value in American society. A social work ethic deduced from this value states, "The social worker should obtain informed consent of clients before taping, recording, or permitting third party observation of their activities." (NASW Code of Ethics II H 5.)[1]

Professional ethics are closely related to, but not identical with general societal ethics. Just as social work values are derived from the values held by society, but are not necessarily identical with those values, so professional ethics come from the same sources as societal ethics, but differ from them in important details. There are differences in priorities, emphases, intensities, and applications. One crucial difference is the ethical principle governing the relationship between two people. Both ethical systems stress the principle of equality, but professional ethics gives priority to the client's interests ahead of the interests of all others.

For social workers this professional ethics principle finds clear expression in at least two paragraphs of the NASW Code of Ethics (see Appendix B, Sections II F and II G). The implications of this

---

[1] See Chapter 3 for a discussion of the dilemmas inherent in the ethic of informed consent.

Interpersonal Relations

GENERAL ETHICS: All persons shall be treated equally.
PROFESSIONAL ETHICS: All persons shall be treated
equally, but priority shall be given to the interests of the
client.

professional ethical principle for social workers and their practice
are manifold. Of course, it is often easier to deduce and formulate
an ethical principle than to apply it in practice. Take the situation
facing one social worker:

2.1: Ms. Macedonia and Diana

Ms. Macedonia is a single parent, the mother of three
children ranging in age from seven through sixteen. Diana is
a high school student who received good grades until the
beginning of this school year, but suddenly has lost all interest
in school. Her grades are now failing and for the past three
weeks she has not gone to school at all.

Ms. Macedonia is a clerical worker in the town's only
industry. She leaves for work before her children go to school
and returns home late in the afternoon, hours after school is
over. Ms. Macedonia manages to keep her home in good
shape. She has no friends in town and always stays by herself.

Recently Ms. Macedonia turned to the family service
agency, indicating that she feels depressed since she does not
know what to do with Diana. The social worker in meeting
with Ms. Macedonia and Diana learns that Ms. Macedonia
makes Diana stay at home with her every evening and every
weekend, primarily because she, Ms. Macedonia, feels lonely.
Many times Diana had wanted to go out with her friends, but
her mother never allowed her to leave.

Who is "the client" to whose interests the social worker
should give priority? Is it Diana? Her mother who made the

initial contact with the agency? Or who? Are there other considerations which might make for an ethical difference?

No profession can establish for itself ethical rules which grossly violate the general ethical standards of the community. If a profession fails to take into consideration the general societal ethic, it risks severe sanction, including the revocation of part or all of its professional authority. Yet society recognizes that practice requirements make it impossible for professionals to follow the identical ethical rules as people generally are expected to observe. Social workers, for example, may ask the kind of questions which in general conversation would be considered inappropriate or even an invasion of privacy. However, before asking such questions the social worker must be certain that asking these questions and obtaining answers is a necessary part of the practice process.

Society does set limits to what social workers may do. And these limits can add to the ethical problems facing the social workers. In many foreign countries, particularly in some of the developing countries, social workers in pursuance of their ethical commitments, have engaged in activities which have placed them in serious conflict with societal ethics. Social workers in several countries, including the Philippines, Chile, Uganda, India and elsewhere, have been jailed because they chose to follow a practice modality and a professional ethic which was contrary to societal expectations. Their fate highlights the fact that ethical problems in professional practice are real and can result in real and even tragic consequences. In this country, some social workers have lost their jobs, have not received promotions, or have been blackballed as a result of acting in accord with their professional ethical principles.

WHO NEEDS PROFESSIONAL ETHICS?

There are those who question the need for professional ethics. Some argue that "common sense" or "practice wisdom" is all that a social worker needs in order to make the right decision, even when facing the most complicated dilemma. The importance of common sense or practice wisdom should not be underrated, but every social worker will recall occasions when these simply were not enough. There are a number of specific arguments against the development and utilization of professional ethics which will be considered here briefly.

1. **Philosophers' Argument.** At least since Aristotle's days philosophers have been unable to agree whether it is possible to determine the truth of ethical principles. As long as it is not possible to develop proof which will establish the correctness of an ethical position, it is best not to fool ourselves into believing that we know what is "right."

2. **Relativity Argument.** What is thought to be "right" varies in different countries and at different times. In one society it is rude to come late for an appointment, in another it is rude to come on time. Which is correct? Even within American society, different ethnic and cultural groups provide conflicting guidelines to what is "correct." In the social welfare field, for example, the emphasis has shifted in recent years from individual welfare to societal welfare. Which emphasis is "right?" Those arguing this way conclude that there are no fixed ethical principles which hold over time or space. Since everything is relative, there is no way of indicating which choice or option is correct.

3. **"No Time" Argument.** Social work practitioners have no time for drawn out ethical reflections because they must act quickly. They do what they think is best for their clients. A code of abstract ethical principles will not help them.

4. **"Uniqueness of Each Case" Argument.** Every case is different and every client presents a unique problem. It is folly to expect that one code of ethical principles will provide adequate guidance for every situation which faces the social work practitioner.

5. **Clinical Argument.** Correct practice is based on competence in clinical skills and not on ethical principles. Many so-called ethical problems are really the result of poor clinical practice. Good contracting will avoid many problems which are presented as ethical problems. By becoming more competent a clinician, the social worker will learn to make appropriate ethical decisions.

6. **Coercion.** There is a latent, if not overt, coercion on the professional to act only in accordance with the provisions of the code of ethics. Such coercion contradicts the basic social work and

democratic value of self-determination. In addition a code of ethics tends to stifle creativity because it places every social worker into the same mold.

These six arguments point to some significant limitations inherent in most codes of professional ethics, but they have not been widely accepted and have not stopped the development of a code. Despite the fact that many social workers face ethical problems almost daily, many have been unwilling to think through the ethical issues involved. For them and for others a code of ethics can provide helpful guidelines for making ethical decisions. In the health care field there has been a similar unwillingness to face ethical problems; this has led to the rise of the new professional specialty of "moral specialist" or "medical ethicist." Social workers, who often face ethical decisions which are as difficult and as fateful as those faced by physicians, have thus far successfully avoided assigning ethical dilemmas to specialists. Decisions around child placement, adoption, or child abuse may be as fateful, or even more so, as determining the exact moment of clinical death. In fact, it has been said that in social work there is no major professional or clinical problem which does not involve ethical issues, and social workers, whether they are aware of it or not, constantly make decisions which have ethical implications.

Current assessment methods may not be sufficiently precise to determine with any degree of certitude or finality the correctness of an ethical position, but this methodological problem does not absolve social workers from continuing to search for the correct path. It may not be possible to identify the one correct way of doing things because various cultural groups in American society define what is right and good in diverse ways. Yet there is need to have a professional consensus on what is expected of a social worker in this society. Once this has been achieved, it should be possible to explore whether there exists among all ethnic and cultural groups a common basis for understanding the right and the good.

Anyone who has practiced social work knows that social workers do not have time for drawn-out theoretical debates, but ethical decisions need not take a long time. And precisely because they have little time, social workers need help in making correct choices.

Similarly, every social worker knows that each case is unique and different, but there are commonalities and these are important. Any significant advance in professional practice will require a better understanding of the common elements. Ethical codes addressed to the common elements will, of course, require adjustment for the unique features of each situation. Finally, the free acceptance of a professional discipline cannot be considered a violation of the self-determination principle. We must conclude, therefore, that the objections raised fail to support the contention that social workers do not need a code of ethics, even if such a code does not supply all the answers which contemporary social workers need.

CODE OF PROFESSIONAL ETHICS

Every occupation which strives to achieve professional status is expected to develop a code of professional ethics. Such a code contains a compilation of the ethical principles relevant to the profession, the principles which members of that profession are expected to maintain. Many professional codes also describe the sanctions which will be employed against those who are not able to meet these expectations. In short, a code attempts to translate professional values into behavioral expectations.

The code of ethics of almost every modern profession has been designed to fill the following functions:

1. Provide practitioners with ethical guidance for practice decisions.

2.. Provide protection for clients and potential clients who have no way of assessing a professional's integrity and competence.

3. Regulate the behavior of professionals and their relations with clients, colleagues, other professionals, employers (if employed), and the community.[2]

---

[2] Earlier codes also attempted to regulate the behavior of clients. Thus, the 1847 Code of the American Medical Association demanded that "obedience of the patient to the prescriptions of his physician should be prompt and implicit. He should never permit his own crude opinion as to their fitness influence his attention to them." Modern codes no longer attempt to control clients' behaviors since they are addressed to professionals, and not to clients or patients.

4. Provide a basis for the appraisal and evaluation of the professional's activities.

Since a code of professional ethics tries to provide guidance for every conceivable situation, it is written in terms of general principles, not specific rules. Yet when comparing earlier with later codes, the tendency to become more specific and to cover a greater variety of specific situations is noticeable. Contrast the 1967 NASW Code of Ethics with that adopted in 1979. The earlier version had many fewer paragraphs and was written in a much more generalized style than the later document. And the same holds true for the codes of other professions.[3] One consequence of this greater detail and greater specification is the increased possibility of internal inconsistencies, that is, the possibility for conflict between various provisions of the same code. These conflicting demands often make for the kind of ethical dilemma which we will discuss in greater detail in the next chapter.

Codes of ethics generally provide guidance only for good/bad decisions. They are far less effective in helping professionals make decisions of the good/good or bad/bad variety. But it is precisely these latter types of decisions which face the social worker most often. Good/bad decisions are those where one of the two options has been accepted as correct, while the other is widely assessed as incorrect or bad. Good/good decisions, on the other hand, are those where all of the options are beneficial, while bad/bad decisions are those where all options result in undesirable consequences (Keith-Lucas 1977:350). The exemplar of John Miller (2.2) typifies an ethical dilemma which is not of the good/bad variety.

2.2: John Miller's return to State Hospital

John Miller is mentally ill and has been so diagnosed by a psychiatrist. For the past three years this twenty-one-year-old young adult has lived at home with his elderly parents. He can

---

[3] The American Medical Association in 1980 adopted a new code of ethics which appears to be a much briefer document than its previous code. One of the reasons for the lack of detail in the new code, according to newspaper reports, is the desire to prevent lengthy litigation which resulted from the previous code. See *New York Times*, July 23, 1980.

take care of his own minimal needs, but takes no interest whatsoever in anyone or anything. Most of every day he sits in the living room, staring into empty space. His parents dare not leave him at home alone. They have approached you, John's social worker, requesting that he be returned to the State Hospital where he has spent most of his life. They feel that they can no longer give him the care he needs.

You know that it is unethical to deprive anyone, even a mentally ill person, of his freedom except under certain clearly specified circumstances. What are the circumstances which would warrant a social worker to consider involuntary hospitalization? Is the parents' consent sufficient? Can you find support for the course of action you recommend in the NASW Code?

How would the ethical dilemma facing this social worker differ if the psychiatric diagnosis indicated that John's symptoms were such as to predict that sooner or later he would inflict serious harm on others, even though so far he has been entirely harmless?

BASIC ETHICAL ISSUES IN SOCIAL WORK: FREEDOM AND POWER

The basic ethical dilemma in social work practice arises out of two, at times contradictory, professional obligations which all social workers have accepted. These are:

1. The obligation to provide professional help when this is needed or requested.

2. The obligation not to interfere with a client's freedom. These professional obligations are almost identical with Gewirth's (1978:64) basic or generic rights of "well-being" and "freedom." In the ideal of all worlds, there is no contradiction between these two rights, but what if a person's well-being can be achieved only at the expense of that person's freedom? Who defines well-being? Who defines the need for professional help? Who can legitimately request professional help for another?

Ideally, no social worker will want to interfere with any person's freedom. But the general societal ethics already suggest that coercion may be ethically justified when (1) there is a grave threat to basic social values or fundamental social institutions or (2) when there is clear and present danger that irreversible or very great harm will be done or will occur if prompt and positive action is not taken. This second condition is the one most relevant for social workers. Though the statement seems clear, the social worker who tries to apply this condition will discover many ambiguities. What is "clear and present danger"? How can it be demonstrated? When is harm sufficiently serious to warrant coercion? Who may coerce? And how definite must the prevention of harm be to permit the violation of a person's freedom? Consider the questions raised in exemplar 2.3 in connection with hospitalization of the mentally ill.

2.3: Involuntary commitment for the mentally ill

Is it ethical for a social worker to initiate involuntary commitment procedures for a mentally ill person if the person's chances for recovery are better (but not very great) upon receiving treatment in a closed institution? How much better must the chances be before the social worker can proceed?

Would the ethical problem be the same if the client were a teenage drug addict?

A social worker's obligation to protect a client's freedom goes beyond the negative injunction not to interfere with the client's freedom. It must also include positive steps which will strengthen or promote the client's freedom. If promoting and not interfering with a client's freedom is to be more than empty rhetoric, social workers must be clear as to what freedom means in this context. A person can be said to be free only when all of the following conditions prevail:

1.   The environment provides a set of options from which a choice can be made.

2.   There is no coercion on the person from any source to choose a specific option.

3.   The person is aware of the set of options available.

4.   The person has sufficient information about the costs and consequences of each option to assess them realistically.

5. The person has the capacity and/or initiative to make a decision on the basis of this assessment.

6. The person has the opportunity to act on the basis of this choice.

Even a superficial examination of reality will confirm that the freedom of most social work clients is limited. While, relatively speaking, Americans may enjoy more freedom than many others, the structural conditions of contemporary society, especially those conditions which reinforce inequality and racism, limit the freedom of most people. Social workers are ethically committed to use their professional skill and know-how to combat racism and all other forms of inequality in order to help all people gain full freedom. Many social workers have been in the forefront of those struggling for more freedom and greater equality for all Americans.

But do social workers understand that the imbalance of power between client and social worker is another factor which limits freedom? Many clients come from powerless social groups, while the social worker often functions as the agent of the power establishment. Much rarer are situations where the client is more powerful than the social worker. But regardless of the initial situation, clients often make themselves vulnerable and give power and a measure of control over themselves to the social worker by revealing the most private parts of their personal lives or potentially damaging information about themselves, their families, or communities. And this situation occurs in social work with groups and communities as well as with individuals and families. In addition, many clients blindly accept their social workers' suggestions in order to win their workers' approval. A social worker may unknowingly widen the power gap by exercising control through verbal or nonverbal messages which solicit certain information during an interview and inhibit other disclosures. Even the "grunting technique" used by a nondirective social worker may result in limiting a client's freedom. This power imbalance between client and worker is real and creates a basic ethical problem. The first step toward coming to grips with this ethical dilemma is to be alert to it. In Chapter 5 we will discuss other suggestions which social workers may want to utilize when faced by this and other ethical dilemmas.

A BRIEF HISTORY OF CODES
OF PROFESSIONAL ETHICS

In an attempt to regulate the relations between professionals and clients and to protect the exploitation of the latter, all modern professions have developed codes of professional ethics. These became popular only in the past one hundred years, but their long and checkered history goes back to the ancient Greeks. Several thousand years ago Hippocrates demanded that Greek physicians pledge themselves to a high level of professional conduct. There is no record of similar codes for theologians and lawyers, the only other professions of antiquity. But the Hippocratic oath became a guide for the correct professional conduct of medical doctors in many parts of the ancient and medieval world.

Just as medicine was the first profession with a code of ethics in antiquity, so did it lead the way in modern times. In England, Dr. Thomas Percival prepared the first of the modern professional codes of ethics in 1803. The first American code was promulgated by the American Medical Association in 1847 and was modeled on Percival's code. Pharmacists followed a few years later with their first code; contemporary accounts suggest that evidently they thought it important that the public differentiate their work and professional conduct from that of physicians.

But for most American occupations the development of codes of ethics coincided, more or less, with their development as a profession. Social workers were aware long before the appearance of Greenwood's article (1957) on the attributes of a profession that a code of ethics was one of the prerequisites for professional recognition. Within a decade of Flexner's jarring pronouncement in 1915 that social work was not yet a profession, social workers, individually and in groups, started to draft professional ethics codes. An "experimental draft code of ethics for social case workers," printed in 1920, has been attributed to Mary Richmond (Pumphrey 1959:11). If dated correctly, this represents the earliest known draft of a code of ethics for social workers.

The prestigious *Annals of the American Society for Political and Social Sciences* devoted its entire May 1922 issue to the subject of ethical codes in the professions and in business. Contemporary observers viewed the appearance of this issue as the crucial trigger event in the emerging interest in such codes. The *Annals* article on social work ethics was written by Mary Van Kleek and Graham R. Taylor, two veteran and highly respected social workers. They reported that social work did not have a written code of professional ethics, but that, nevertheless, social work pràctice was guided by the ideal of service and not by any thought of financial gain.

Yet the time was ripe for an ethical code for social workers. Several local and national groups developed draft codes within the next few years. In 1923 the American Association for Organizing Family Social Work prepared, but did not adopt, a detailed draft code. Many of the thirty-eight paragraphs of that code reappeared in subsequent drafts and still sound relevant today.

The American Association of Social Workers (AASW), the largest professional social work organization of that day, came out in favor of a code of professional ethics. An editorial in the April 1924 issue of *The Compass*, the official journal of the AASW, asked, "Hasn't the public a right to know how the ordinary social worker is likely to act under ordinary circumstances?" The Research Committee of AASW undertook an inquiry among the chapters to identify common problems of ethical practice. Before this study was completed, the AASW Executive Committee appointed a National Committee on Professional Ethics. This action spurred many local chapters to discuss the need for a code. Several chapters tried to produce draft documents. The Toledo, Ohio, AASW chapter reportedly was the first local chapter to publicize a draft code. Though the Toledo draft was very brief and limited to a few general principles, it inspired others to try their hand at preparing a draft code of professional ethics. However, despite much local interest in some places—how widespread the interest was is not known—the adoption of a national professional code had to await further organizational developments. Only in 1951 did the AASW Delegate Assembly adopt a code of ethics, but this code applied only to affiliated caseworkers.

When the historic merger of all professional social work organizations occurred in the mid-fifties, work on drafting a new code of professional ethics for all social workers was started almost immediately, but it was not until 1960 that the Delegate Assembly adopted such a code. Seven years later this code was amended to include a nondiscrimination principle. The absence of a nondiscrimination provision from earlier codes tells much about the change in the moral climate of this country.

Before long there were calls for a complete revision of the code in order to produce a document which would provide clearer guidance for practitioners and which would be more in tune with the realities of contemporary society. A completely new code was adopted by the 1979 Delegate Assembly of the NASW (see Appendix B). Apparently even the present code does not yet provide sufficient guidance for social work practitioners who seek help when facing difficult ethical problems since calls for yet another revision were heard even before the present code was adopted.

The revised NASW Code of Ethics has placed a much greater emphasis on the welfare of individuals than did the 1967 Code. This change is problematic. A content analysis of many different codes of professional ethics found that, except for the medical profession, all of the helping professions have placed a greater emphasis on the common welfare than have social workers (Howe 1980). At least one group of social workers, those affiliated with the National Association of Black Social Workers, have prepared another code of ethics. This code gives expression to their belief that an individual's welfare can be served best by promoting the common welfare of all Black people (see Appendix B).

SUMMARY

The conflict between freedom and well-being is not a new twentieth century phenomenon. In every age there have been professionals who have tried to wrestle with the ethical dilemma arising out of this conflict. At times these questions were discussed in the academies, at other times written codes of professional ethics have resulted. The chances for making ethical errors remain, even for those who engage seriously in the examination of these ethical questions. Despite this risk, social workers must make an honest effort to face the ethical dilemmas inherent in their practice. In professional ethics there are no easy answers, yet this must not serve as an excuse for avoiding a commitment to ethical practice.

EXERCISES

1. Ethical statements are derived from values. Identify the relevant social work ethic for the following societal values:

  cultural diversity
  equality
  freedom
  integrity
  knowledge building
  privacy
  social justice

2. Cite an historical or contemporary example of a social worker who has suffered because he or she acted in accord with professional ethical principles. Hint: you might start your search by reading current issues of the *NASW News* or *Social Work*. Other sources you might want to search include *Social Work Research and Abstracts*, the *New York Times Index* or *Readers Guide to Periodical Literature*.

3. Review the six "conditions for freedom" cited in this chapter. What specific actions can you take (or suggest) to increase the freedom of your clients?

3 Professional Dilemmas in Postindustrial Society

A dilemma is a problem situation or predicament which seems to defy a satisfactory solution. The word *dilemma* comes from two Greek roots: *di* (double) and *lemma* (proposition). A dilemma is a predicament in which the decision maker must choose between two options of near or equal value. In addition, the dilemmas which confront modern professionals may result from options which are not well defined or from solutions which create additional problems and harm for the problem carrier or for others.

Professional dilemmas are the ethical predicaments which professionals face in their practice. Strictly speaking, it would be more correct to speak of the ethical aspects of problem situations which professionals face, rather than of ethical dilemmas. In this vein, the German philosopher Friedrich Nietzsche noted (1923:91) that "there is no such thing as a moral phenomenon, but only a moral interpretation of phenomena." Nevertheless, we will continue to talk about ethical problems and ethical dilemmas in order to highlight that aspect of the decision-making process on which this book focuses. But it must be remembered that the ethical aspect is only one variable of many which social workers must take into consideration when making professional practice decisions.

Some have suggested that social workers are especially prone to ethical dilemmas because the problems with which they deal are by nature ambiguous. But an examination of many professions has revealed that ethical dilemmas are generic to all professionals who practice in postindustrial societies. In the last chapter the two core sources for the modern professional's predicament were identified as the freedom/well-being dichotomy and the worker/client power gap. A number of specific professional dilemmas will be discussed in somewhat greater detail in this chapter. These are derived from or affected by the core dilemmas. The exemplars in each instance will come from social work practice, though the dilemmas are of much wider significance. Elsewhere many of the same dilemmas were utilized to identify problem situations faced by other professionals, such as nurses (Loewenberg, forthcoming). Since the dilemmas are applicable to all contemporary professions, they will first be formulated on a high level of generality.

PROFESSIONAL DILEMMAS

1. **Ambiguity and Uncertainty.** Making professional decisions without precisely knowing what the consequences of such choices will be.

2. **Conflicting Obligations and Expectations.** Making professional decisions in the face of multiple, often conflicting obligations, demands, and expectations, coming from many different role opposites, including clients, colleagues, supervisors, employers, society and others.

3. **Professional Knowledge/Client's Rights.** Making professional decisions on the basis of one's professional knowledge and experience, even while respecting the right of clients to choose what they believe is best for them.

4. **Informed Consent.** Making professional decisions based on the client's informed consent, even while realizing that clients rarely understand all the implications and consequences of the choices facing them.

5. **Sharing Limited Resources.** Making professional decisions on the basis of sharing limited resources equally among all clients to whom one has a professional obligation, even while realizing that a specific client needs a much greater share of these resources.

6. **Priority of Client's Interests/Worker's Interests.** Making professional decisions on the basis of what is best for the client, even

if the worker's job or life may be at stake as a consequence of such a choice.

7. Choice of Effective Interventive Methods. Making professional decisions on the basis of one's own expertise, even while another modality (in which the worker is less expert) may be more effective for a given problem situation or a particular client.

8. Limited Nature of the Professional Relationship. Making professional decisions which permit only the use of the limited professional relationship, even though the client really needs a total relationship.

9. Suspension of Judgment. Making professional decisions on the basis of suspending one's value judgment, even when one's own values or societal values clearly indicate a preference or demand a judgment.

As social workers make ethical decisions they will face additional dilemmas. This list includes the most common types of professional dilemmas. A more detailed examination of these dilemmas, together with exemplars for discussion, follows.

DILEMMA 1

Ambiguity and Uncertainty

Two types of ambiguity and uncertainty make for ethical problems in social work practice:

1. Uncertainty about values and goals.
2. Uncertainty about the consequences of the social worker's intervention.

These two types of uncertainty occur in a world which is characterized by a general disillusionment with all kinds of authority. The infallible guides and granite virtues of yesteryear have been discarded like last season's fashion. Even the faith in science and progress, characteristic of the belief system of a more recent era, has moved from center stage and has been replaced by a pervasive sense of ambiguity and uncertainty. The pursuit of personal happiness and fulfillment has replaced other ethical imperatives, making it more and more difficult to know objectively what is right. In fact, some contemporary philosophers have suggested that one's own idea of good is what is right. But those who have accepted this relativistic philosophy find that they too must cope with ambiguity and uncertainty, just as much as those who are still searching for ethical imperatives which are relevant in contemporary society.

Ambiguity may be a greater problem for social workers than for other professionals because social work practice occurs under conditions where the practitioner has even less control over the outcome of the intervention than most other professionals. The issues with which social workers deal are by nature vague. The level of available social work knowledge does not give the practitioner the same type of knowledge base that many of the more established professions have been able to provide for their practitioners. And perhaps most important, so many different factors impinge simultaneously on the human being that it is difficult for the social worker to assess the specific impact of the intervention. An unsuccessful outcome may be (but need not be) due to something the social worker did or did not do. The same intervention activity in two seemingly identical problem situations may lead to two entirely different outcomes because of factors over which the social worker has no control.

A social worker usually does not know to what extent his or her intervention has made or will make a difference because so many other factors come into play. In addition, little will be known about what would have happened if the social worker had not intervened or had utilized a different strategy. In case of suspected child abuse, a social worker cannot predict with certainty what will happen if the child stays with its parents, nor will the worker be able to know positively what might happen if the child were forcibly removed (see exemplar 3.1). Similarly, no social worker can predict with any accuracy whether helping a neighborhood council obtain a grant for restoring dilapidated houses is the best or the worst help that could be offered. And yet, in spite of the ambiguities of the situation and the uncertainties caused by lack of knowledge, every social worker must act.

3.1:   Leroy Hill, victim of child abuse

Several months ago Ms. Gillis told her public welfare social worker that she suspected that her upstairs neighbor, Mr. Hill, regularly and brutally beat his two-year-old son Leroy. She would hear the most frightful noises several evenings a week, but saw the boy only at very rare intervals. When she did see him, he always wore bandages and looked so sad. The worker noted these remarks in her case report, but took no further action.

Last month Ms. Hill brought Leroy to Lakeside General Hospital emergency room. Leroy suffered from multiple fractures which, according to his mother, occurred when he fell down the front stairs. The attending physician did not believe her story since the X-ray revealed a large number of previous fractures in addition to the current ones. As required by law he notified the public welfare department that he suspected child abuse.

As a result of the physician's report, Andre Conti, an experienced social worker, was sent to the Hill home to investigate. After talking extensively with both parents he concluded that the boy was in no immediate danger.

Two weeks later, a second social worker made a follow-up visit to the Hills. This worker, Millie Walker, agreed with Mr. Conti's assessment that there was no need to remove Leroy from his home.

Ten days after Ms. Walker's visit, Ms. Hill called for an emergency ambulance, saying that her baby was having difficulties breathing. When the ambulance crew arrived, they found that Leroy was unconscious. Twelve hours after he was brought to the hospital, he was pronounced dead without recovering consciousness. The cause of death, according to the death certificate, was severe beating.

This exemplar gives rise to a number of ethical questions. These include the following: Was Ms. Gillis' social worker right in not doing anything about the child abuse report? Are a neighbor's suspicions sufficient cause to warrant interfering in the Hill family? How can Mr. Conti or any social worker establish that "a clear and present danger" exists for Leroy's life? When does parental discipline become child abuse? Should Mr. Conti have talked with Ms. Gillis before deciding what to recommend about Leroy? Under what conditions is the removal of a child from the family justified? Can a child be removed without its parents' consent? When? How certain must the social worker be of the consequences of leaving a child and/or the consequences of removing a child from the home?

Note that there are two sets of ambiguities in the Leroy Hill exemplar: those arising out of lack of clarity of societal norms (What are the limits of parental disciplining?) and those arising out of lack of knowledge (What evidence is sufficient? What are the consequences?). The social workers involved in this case made professional judgments that Leroy was not "at risk," but their judgment was mistaken. As a consequence Leroy died. But before condemning these workers, it should be realized that the mistake could also have gone in the other direction—finding a risk when there was no risk and thus removing the boy from his home needlessly.

Ambiguities and uncertainties are endemic conditions in social work. An effective social worker retains the ability to function even while coping with these ethical dilemmas. Compare this with F. Scott Fitzgerald's (1936) observation that "The test of a first-rate intelligence is the ability to hold two opposed ideas in the mind at the same time and still retain the ability to function."

DILEMMA 2

Conflicting Obligations and Expectations

Social workers, like other contemporary professionals, must deal with dilemmas arising out of role conflict and role-set conflict. Role conflict occurs because a person occupies many different role positions simultaneously. For example, Andre Conti (exemplar 3.1) was at one and the same time a social worker, father, husband, son, son-in-law, Black, Democrat, Unitarian, and ham radio operator. He faces different obligations in each of these roles. His wife expects him to spend evenings with her at home, while his friends expect him to participate in the frequent political rallies in the months prior to the elections. Role-set conflict, on the other hand, arises out of conflicting expectations which different role opposites have from the occupier of a given role position. Clients, colleagues, and supervisor each have different expectations of what Andre Conti should do as a social worker. Here the conflict is not between the different roles which one person fills, but between the varying expectations which different people have from the same role. The dilemmas arising out of role-set conflict will be analyzed in this section, while some aspects of role conflict will be discussed in Section 6 below.

The answer to the question, "Who is the client?" is a major issue in the dilemma of conflicting obligations. Traditionally, a client was defined as the person(s) who engaged the professional and paid the fee or the person (or system) who was to be modified or changed by the professional's intervention. However, most social workers are employed and paid by a social agency, a department of government, or an institution. Does this mean that the agency, government, or the institution is their client? Does the school become the client of the school social worker? Is the prison the client of the correctional social worker? The traditional definition may be too narrow, and useful only for self-employed professionals. The second part of the definition also presents problems since it is not always correct to say that the client is the person or system which is to be changed. Often the social work intervention involves changes in systems other than the client. When a social worker helps a recently widowed woman qualify for social security benefits, the worker does not change the client, but instead helps the client to change her environment. Until not too long ago, a surgeon was certain that the sick person who wanted an operation was the patient, just as the social worker considered the person(s) who applied for help as the client. However, today neither physician nor social worker are entirely certain that the answer to the question "Who is the client?" is quite so simple, as the following two exemplars will illustrate.

3.2: Arlene Johnson's abortion

Arlene Johnson, eighteen years old and unmarried, is nearly six months pregnant. She came to the Women's Counseling Center (WCC) to request an abortion. Robin

Osborn was assigned as her social worker. Because of the advanced phase of pregnancy, the intake process was reduced to a minimum and Ms. Johnson was referred to Community Hospital instead of the clinic to which WCC clients are usually referred.

The abortion was performed within forty-eight hours after Ms. Johnson first contacted WCC. At the time of delivery the foetus was considered viable and was placed in the neonatal intensive care unit as a high risk premature baby.

Arlene was most upset when she learned that the abortion had resulted in a live infant. She refused to look at her baby. Instead, she threatened to sue the doctor and the hospital if the infant survived despite her expressed wish.

Arlene then asked Ms. Osborn, her social worker, to support her desire that the baby not be given intensive care, but rather be left alone so that it would die.

3.3: Mrs. Linden's classroom

Mrs. Linden is a fifth-grade teacher in P.S. 34. The school is located in a neighborhood which recently witnessed the influx of a large number of Puerto Rican families. Mrs. Ramirez has been assigned as school social worker to this school.

Yesterday Mrs. Linden asked Mrs. Ramirez for help in keeping her pupils in their seats, working quietly. She told Mrs. Ramirez that never in her twenty years as a teacher has she had as much trouble as this year. She thought that her trouble was due to the many children who had transferred from Puerto Rican schools. Surely Mrs. Ramirez could advise her how to handle these children so that they would be quiet and stay in their seats.

The two problem situations seem quite different, but in each the expectation of the applicant for service places the professional before an ethical dilemma. Arlene Johnson does not want to have a baby, but once the foetus was declared viable, Arlene's expectations of the surgeon (and later of the social worker) conflict sharply with the rights of the infant and with society's expectations from these role occupants. Similarly, Mrs. Linden's expectations are different from those of her students. Both teacher and student have different expectations from Mrs. Ramirez. And the social worker is not at all sure that the problem is with the pupils; perhaps the teacher is the problem? Is it really in the pupils' best interest to keep them still and docile? Whose rights (teacher or pupils') take precedence?

Actually, the question "Who is the client?" is based on an oversimplified model of the helping relationship in contemporary society. The traditional model included only the helper (social worker) and the client. But a more realistic and updated model must include, in addition to the social worker and the social agency, the applicant, client, target, and beneficiary. (See boxed-in model.) Each of these latter positions can be occupied by one or more persons

---

Participants In The Social Work Process

Applicant—the person(s) or system who requests help with a defined or felt problem

Client—the applicant who enters into a formal, contractual, goal-focused relationship with the social worker

Target—the person(s) or system who must be modified to achieve the outcome contracted between client and worker

Beneficiary—the person(s) or system who will benefit from successful goal achievement. (Definitions based on Loewenberg 1977:22–23; see also Loewenberg and Dolgoff 1972:261.)

---

or institutions. Sometimes one person is both applicant, client, target and beneficiary. At other times or in other situations different persons or institutions occupy each of these positions. And when this is the case, we can be almost sure that each will have their own expectations of the social worker—and often their expectations conflict, placing the social worker before an ethical dilemma. Whose expectations should receive priority attention? There is little doubt that Arlene Johnson and Mrs. Linden were the applicants, but Robin Osborn, the WCC social worker, and Mrs. Ramirez, the school social worker, faced ethical dilemmas around the question of identifying the primary client, target and beneficiary. For whom do they have primary ethical obligations? The social workers of Ms. Macedonia (exemplar 2.1) and of John Miller (exemplar 2.2) also faced a similar ethical dilemma.

Genetic counseling places social workers before especially difficult problems. Modern genetic testing procedures, such as amniocentesis, make it possible to detect as many as sixty different genetic disorders (including Down's syndrome and Tay–Sach's disease) as early as the fourteenth to sixteenth week of pregnancy. When there is a positive finding, the social worker will want to help the parents think through all of the implications before reaching an informed decision, a decision they think is correct. However, many physicians expect that the social worker will always persuade the pregnant mother to decide to abort the genetically defective foetus. Should the best interest of the as-yet-unborn child play a part in the decision? Should the social worker reinforce arguments in favor of abortion, even if it is evident that the parents' thinking tends to go in the opposite direction? What is the ethical decision here? A further dilemma in these situations relates to the desire of other relatives for access to genetic information which may be of importance to their health or to that of their children. Does their right take precedence over the client's right of privacy?[1]

Social workers in the criminal justice system face the ethical dilemma of conflicting obligations in other ways. In the probation service social workers regularly prepare reports for the juvenile court judge. The judge takes these reports into consideration when making a final disposition of the case. An ethical dilemma arises from the fact that the social worker is both helper and judicial fact-finder. The client-worker relationship starts during the first contact with the juvenile, long before the social worker has completed the evaluative diagnosis or written the report. The exemplar of Warren Duffy's confession is typical of this type of ethical dilemma.

---

[1] See Sammons (1978) for a more detailed discussion of the questions raised here.

3.4:   Warren Duffy's confession

Warren Duffy, a fifteen-year-old six-footer, was charged with armed robbery. In a juvenile court hearing Warren denied the charge, claiming complete innocence, perhaps a case of mistaken identity. He was remanded to Youth House while the charge was investigated. Orlando Corrado was assigned as his social worker.

While evaluating his background, Warren told Mr. Corrado that he did commit the crime with which he is charged. Corrado suggested that it might be best for Warren if he tell the judge what he had told him. Warren refused to do so and added that what he had told the social worker was said in strictest confidence.

The social worker's obligations are clear, but conflicting. Warren expects the social worker to respect his confidence and keep quiet; the judge expects a full and honest report. Orlando Corrado faces an ethical dilemma because he cannot meet both expectations. What arguments can be marshalled in favor of each expectation? Note that the ethical question is not what the social worker should do once a decision has been made, but rather how to resolve the ethical dilemma. If, for example, Orlando decides that he has an ethical obligation to the judge (or to society) to report what he has learned from Warren about the criminal act, then there are a number of good-practice activities which he might undertake, including discussing his decision and the reasons for it with Warren.

The situation is different for social workers who are not connected with the criminal justice system, but the dilemma of conflicting obligations is just as real when they become aware of law violations. The case of a suspected welfare fraud is typical of this kind of ethical dilemma.

3.5:   Suspected welfare fraud

Jean Fisher is a marriage counselor and family therapist in the Old Towne Family Consultation Center, a nonsectarian United Chest agency. Sue and Dean Kern have been coming to her for family therapy once a week for the past two months.

While their problem was not critical, they came to seek help while the marriage was still salvageable.

During today's sesssion Dean Kern mentioned that he has been receiving SSI support payments for his aged mother who used to live with them, but who two years ago moved overseas to live with her other daughter.

Should Ms. Fisher report this case of possible welfare fraud? Or is this situation covered by client-worker confidentiality? What will happen to the client-therapist relationship if Ms. Fisher does report what she has learned? Should she consider the possible consequences to treatment before she decides what to do?

What would be Ms. Fisher's obligation if she had learned that Dean Kern had robbed a bank? Or was planning to rob a bank? Or that Sue Kern was pushing drugs? Does the seriousness of the offense change the ethical considerations? Does the degree of harm the offense might cause make a difference?

Sometimes differences in expectations occur because various role opposites occupy different status positions. One can understand that adolescents and adults, offenders and judges, pupils and teachers view the world in different ways, each from their own perspective. Sometimes lack of consensus arises out of cultural differences or (what in an earlier period was known as) the culture gap. In periods of rapid social change this type of ethical dilemma becomes particularly acute and frequent. It was commonplace for social workers in recent decades to face violently conflicting expectations from different participants around situations involving alternate life styles.

Social agencies claim to be value-free and dedicated to serving the best interests of their clients, but many if not most are in fact an integral part of the organized and established community, serving (knowingly or unknowingly) the interests of that community as defined by important decision makers. Agency services, locations, budget allocations, personnel hirings and assignments, and other arrangements serve to reinforce agency commitments, whatever these are. Serious ethical dilemmas face social workers who honestly want to serve their clients' best interests, but are constrained by their obligations to the agency. This type of dilemma frequently occurs when social workers become involved (or want to become involved) in advocacy service or in empowerment, but it also occurs in connection with purely technical and apolitical decisions, such as the choice of an effective intervention modality, as the following exemplar demonstrates.

3.6:   Dr. Henrique's drinking problem

Cele Henrique, M.D., immigrated from Cuba three years ago. Neither she nor her physician-husband have yet qualified to practice medicine in this state. Cele has become increasingly frustrated by her low-status job as a medical technician. In Cuba they were on the top of the social ladder; here their lifestyle is very restricted and they feel as if they are close to the the bottom of the social ladder. Cele Henrique has turned to alcohol for relief from her frustrations.

Some months ago her husband left her. Soon thereafter Cele increased her consumption of alcohol. When she was unable to retain her job because she missed so many days, she realized that she had a problem for which she needed professional help. She turned to the Valley Alcohol Detoxification Center, the only alcohol treatment program in this part of the state. Edna Teague, a social worker in this program, was on intake duty when Dr. Henrique walked in.

As a result of the intake interview, Edna Teague felt that an individual therapy program would be most effective. However, since the state legislature made budgetary cuts last year, the center offers only group counseling. Edna Teague is convinced that Dr. Henrique will not benefit from a group program.

A social worker's professional obligations conflict with her obligations to her employer. Edna Teague might have been able to avoid this dilemma if she could have referred Dr. Henrique to another agency which offers individual therapy, but in the present instance there was no other agency that offered this service. In long range terms, Mrs. Teague may want to participate in changing agency policy or budget allocations, but this will be of no immediate help for Dr. Henrique—and Dr. Henrique needs help now.

The last type of conflicting obligations dilemma to be discussed here might be called the case of negative conflict. This occurs when a social worker, because of professional or ideological commitments, does not want to meet the expectations of one role opposite, but does want to meet the identical expectations of another role opposite. Many poor residents of the Black ghetto or Chicano barrio desire family planning services, just as do people who live in other neighborhoods. But the social worker also knows that powerful racist groups in the community give financial support to the voluntary family planning program because they want to reduce the birth rate of minority groups. What is this social worker to to do? Is it ethical to serve one's clients, knowing that this program will also serve the antisocial goals of other participants?

DILEMMA 3

Professional Knowledge/Client's Rights

Social workers firmly believe that all persons have the right to make their own decisions. Towle accurately assessed this stance when she wrote (1965:18), "the client's right to self-determination was one of the first, if not the first, of our beliefs to become a banner around which we rallied." At the same time, professional social work is based on the premise that social workers can, and (when asked to) have an obligation, to help people. Professional social work help is based on a body of professional knowledge, a set of professional values, and various professional skills which have been developed over the years and which social workers acquire in professional education programs, as well as on the job.

Social workers believe that they will not be helpful (or will be less helpful) if they do not utilize this professional knowledge and the appropriate professional skills, but the professional helping strategy may be severely limited when the client makes decisions which conflict with what the professional thinks is best. The social worker may know what strategy will best achieve the objectives which the client has chosen, but may the social worker implement this strategy if the client prefers another? The social worker may understand what it is that the client wants, even though the client is not yet aware of what might be best for him or her. Again the question arises: may the social worker follow professional knowledge and insight, even if the client has made another, less beneficial decision, based on ignorance or partial knowledge? Halmos (1965:92), asking these same questions, observed that the therapist can hardly expect to be helpful "unless we mean therapy to be therapeutic and, therefore, determining and directing in important ways." Others argue that a social worker must never make decisions for the client. Yet no matter whose lead we follow, the clash between the firm belief in the client's right to self-determination at all times, on the one hand, and the use of professional knowledge and skills to direct the helping effort, on the other, results in the third ethical dilemma, an ethical dilemma which all social workers face frequently. If they fully respect the client's right to make decisions, no matter how faulty they may be, there is danger that social workers will cease to practice on a professional level and instead become mere paper pushers. But if they infringe on the client's right to make decisions when professional practice demands make this advisable, they apparently violate a basic tenet of the professional ethic. This appears to be a no-win situation.

There are, of course, many situations where a social worker can follow the best of practice knowledge and professional skills and still fully respect a client's right to self-determination. One of the reasons for this is that social workers believe not only in the right, but also in the therapeutic effect of client participation in all phases of the social work process. They have moved a long way from what was the traditional professional position which, in the words of the 1847 AMA Code of Ethics, declared that professionals had "a right to expect and require that their patients should entertain a just sense of duties which they owe to their medical attendants." Early social workers may not have been as blatant in their public statements, but they too expected that clients follow their good advice without too many questions. No wonder that there developed the feeling that professionals really cared only about their own welfare. G. B. Shaw in *Preface to The Doctor's Dilemma* expressed this feeling when he said that "all professions are conspiracies against the laity." This antiprofessional feeling still is prevalent in our days.

In the 1960s and 1970s, one of the arguments used by those who wanted to diminish the influence of professional social workers by promoting indigenous workers was precisely the argument that professionalism resulted in a neglect of citizen participation in decision-making.

The conflict between client self-determination and the worker's use of professional knowledge and skill need not be Machiavellian. Even when social workers care about their clients' interests and about their rights, they may face this ethical dilemma, as the worker of Eleanor Pomer (exemplar 3.7) discovered.

3.7:   Should Eleanor Pomer come home?

Eleanor Pomer is an eight-year-old Black girl, the youngest of six siblings. For the past three years she has been a resident in a special school because of a diagnosis of Down's syndrome. According to her cottage parents, her psychologist, her teachers, and her social worker, she functions on a moderately retarded level.

Both of Eleanor's parents are employed. They rent the downstairs apartment of a two-family home in a working class neighborhood, about one hour's drive from Eleanor's school. Mr. and Mrs. Pomer visit Eleanor about once a month. For the past year-and-a-half Eleanor has spent one weekend a month at home.

Eleanor's home visits have been successful. Both Eleanor and her family look forward to these monthly visits. The school's staff now feels that Eleanor is ready to leave the school and live again at home. The social worker has acquainted Eleanor's parents with this staff assessment, has told them about community resources which are available in their city, and has urged them to take Eleanor home. However, the Pomers are satisfied with the present arrangement, feeling that it would be too much of a strain on their other children if Eleanor lived at home again.

The social worker is convinced that it would be best for Eleanor to leave the school and resume a more normal home life. Eleanor is excited about the possibility of living again with her parents and brothers and sisters.

This social worker faces a number of dilemmas, arising out of the conflict between professional knowledge and the client's right to make decisions. How much weight should the social worker give to the Pomers' wishes? To Eleanor's wish? Should what is best for Eleanor be the only or the most important criterion in reaching a decision? Does the social worker have an ethical right to manipulate the environment (for example, by raising the tuition fee) in order to "help" the Pomers reach the decision which is best for Eleanor? A social worker does not always know best, but sometimes the worker does know more about some things than the client. Often the worker feels obligated to provide the client with information in order that the client can reach a better decision. But when the social worker gives information, the client may believe that the worker is indicating a preference. Or by helping a client clarify a doubt or resolve a confusion, the worker may inadvertently steer toward a certain decision. The ethical social worker will want to avoid situations which seem to limit client decision-making, but at the same time the worker does have a professional obligation to help. The next exemplar provides an opportunity to analyze another aspect of this dilemma.

3.8: Peggy Nguyen's vague feelings

Peggy Nguyen, twenty-eight years old and married, recently gave birth to a seven pound boy, her third child. Her oldest boy is three and her girl is one year old. Peggy's husband is taking care of the older children while Peggy is in the maternity hospital. The hospital social worker, Nicole Devereaux discussed family planning with Ms. Nguyen, as she does with all mothers. She learned from several conversations that Ms. Nguyen vaguely feels that she has had enough children, but it is quite clear that neither she nor her husband are strongly motivated to limit the family's size.

Should Ms. Devereaux conclude from the client's "vague feelings" that she is asking for help in strengthening her motivation for family planning? Or would this be an unwarranted intrusion by the social worker? Perhaps Ms. Nguyen's problem is one of a lack of knowledge about family limitation methods. Should Ms. Devereaux supply these, even though the client has not requested her to do so? Would Ms. Devereaux be justified in assuming on the basis of her knowledge and experience that Ms. Nguyen's cultural background may make for a problem with family planning? Should she offer the client help in resolving this dilemma?

The clients' right to make their own decisions coincides with the social work value of self-determination. Yet social workers generally agree that self-determination is not an absolute right. Bernstein (1960) wrote that self-determination is "not supreme, but supremely important," and Perlman (1965) suggested that self-determination, though important, was nine-tenths illusion. A number of limitations to the right of client self-determination have been discussed in the professional literature. These include: (1) lack of resources to implement a decision, (2) lack of capacity to make a decision, (3) greater power or knowledge of another person who, knowingly or unknowingly, limits the client's decision-making, and (4) conflicting objectives which may supersede the client's rights, such as the responsibility to prevent harm to that person or to others. More recently some have argued that a social worker has no right to limit a client's decision to harm himself or herself, as long as no other person is injured by such an act. But is it possible for a person to commit suicide or use alcohol excessively without injuring another? If a mother commits suicide, the surviving children will suffer emotional and material harm. If a husband or teenager drinks to excess every night, every member of their family will suffer. The reader is also referred to the next section where this discussion is continued in connection with the question of voluntary and informed consent.

The contractual nature of the social work process also tends to limit the client's right to make decisions. Whatever decisions the client makes concerning social work objectives and strategies require the actual or implicit consent of the social worker before they can be actualized. The social worker has, in effect, a veto power over the client's decisions, just as the client can veto the social worker's decisions by terminating contact. Mr. Pomer (exemplar 3.7) can veto whatever decision the social worker has made concerning his daughter. But must the social worker accept whatever decision Mr. Pomer has made, even if this decision is not in the best interest of his daughter?

DILEMMA 4

Informed Consent

Problems around informed consent are at the very core of many ethical dilemmas. Informed consent, simply put, means that a social worker or another professional will not intervene in a client's life or domain unless the client has consented to such intervention. Informed consent involves questions of *knowledge, voluntariness*, and *competence*. Problems involving any one or all of these elements make for difficult ethical dilemmas in social work practice, as will become evident when we consider the exemplars in this section.

3.9: Archie Walker's golden years

Muriel Palmieri is an outreach worker at the Downtown Elderly Program (DEP). She has organized a group of volunteers who visit regularly with homebound older people. They also have been trained to identify older people who need additional help. One of these volunteers recently told Ms. Palmieri that she had discovered a bedridden old man in a cold and dirty fourth floor walk-up apartment. Archie Walker was probably not as old or as feeble as he appeared, but the volunteer thought that he required more care than the occasional help provided by his seventy-nine-year-old neighbor who brought food whenever he thought of it. When this neighbor forgot to come, as happened not infrequently, Mr. Walker subsisted for days on cold water only. It had been years since Mr. Walker last saw a doctor. He seemed delighted with the volunteer's visit and begged her to come again.

Ms. Palmieri promised the volunteer that she would follow up within a day or two to see what could be done to make Mr. Walker's golden years more comfortable. She did visit Mr. Walker on the following morning and verified the volunteer's report. Mr. Walker seemed relatively alert. The worker thought that his dissatisfaction with his present condition was a hopeful sign, indicative of a capacity to participate in developing plans for his future. Walker explained that his only income came from Social Security. He had never heard of SSI (the Federal Supplementary Security Income Program) though Ms. Palmieri suspected that he could qualify for this program. He said that he could not afford to hire someone to look after him or his apartment. But he was vehement in his insistence that he did not ever want to go to an old folks' home.

Ms. Palmieri, in the course of her visit, explained to Mr. Walker many of the programs which were available to persons in his situation. She noted the advantages and disadvantages of each, indicating the time it might take before the service or program would start for him and what she could and could not do to help him qualify. Among the programs and services she discussed were SSI, meals-on-wheels, Medicaid, health visitor, homemaker, Title 8 housing, The Manor Apartments, and others.

Mr. Walker seemed bewildered by the many choices he had to make. He asked Ms. Palmieri what she thought might be best for him.

If you were in Ms. Palmieri's shoes, what would you have done? Here are some of the questions and issues that Ms. Palmieri thought about as she tried to unravel the dilemma facing her:

1. Did Mr. Walker give his consent so that the social worker could begin to make arrangements for applying for help on his behalf? What does the last sentence in the exemplar mean? Is this a satisfactory way of giving informed consent? If not, in what ways did it fall short of "informed consent"?

2. Should Ms. Palmieri have recognized the client's limited experience in decision-making and instead of overwhelming him with dozens of choices, simplified the decisions to be made by selecting only a few options? Perhaps it would have been better to have Mr. Walker decide first whether he wanted to stay in his present apartment or move somewhere else. But can he make this decision properly without a full knowledge about all of the available options?

3. Ms. Palmieri tried to present all of the advantages and disadvantages of every option. But does she herself really know *all* of the consequences? And does Mr. Walker really care about *all* of the consequences? Is he not much more interested in what will happen to him in the next few months than in any long range consequences?

4. Would it be ethical for Ms. Palmieri to design a package of relevant services on the basis of her diagnosis and on the basis of Mr. Walker's wishes, and then ask Mr. Walker whether or not he agreed with this strategy?

Additional questions could be asked, but it should be clear from the above that in social work practice "informed consent" is beset with many difficulties and that these difficulties often lead to ethical dilemmas. The three components of informed consent, as already noted, are (a) knowledge, (b) voluntariness, and (c) competency. We will discuss briefly the ethical dilemma or dilemmas inherent in each of these components.

a. **Knowledge.** Lack of knowledge has been called the Achilles' heel of informed consent (Bermant et al. 1978:255). Persons cannot be considered sufficiently informed to give consent if they lack knowledge about what will occur during the intervention or treatment, about the results of the intervention, and about the consequences of not giving consent for the intervention. Similar knowledge should be available about all alternate options. Some of this knowledge can be provided by the social worker. But many of the outcomes are unknown even to the social worker. Ms. Palmieri might explain to Mr. Walker how meals-on-wheels operates, the type of food this program provides, and how much it costs. However, she does not know how Mr. Walker's stomach will react to warm food, how long the present cook will stay, or whether this program will survive the next budget cuts. In fact, Mr. Walker may lose the "help" of his neighbor (inadequate as it was) if he joins meals-on-wheels and be in a worse position if that program is ever terminated. Ms. Palmieri might point out all those benefits and risks of which she is aware, but there are always secondary and unanticipated consequences which are virtually unpredictable.

There is also evidence that clients often do not pay attention to the information presented to them. Whether this is a case of selective listening or of suppressing unpleasant information is not certain, but one New York hospital researcher found that no matter how careful doctors were in explaining the details of surgery and the possibility of death or complications, twenty-four hours later most patients were unable to recall accurately for the researcher what they had been told by the doctor. Lest it be thought that patients in this study were not given adequate information before signing the "consent for surgery" form, the informed consent explanations were videotaped and later reviewed by independent judges. Many of the doctors told the researchers that, though they had provided their patients with all available information, they felt that most of the patients simply did not want to know what could go wrong when they went into surgery (*Los Angeles Times* 6/8/80). Social workers differ in many ways from surgeons, but many social workers also report that their clients really do not want to know all the details. They have a problem and want help from an expert whom they trust. Yet the social worker is ethically committed to the principle of informed consent. Here, then, is the root of an ethical dilemma. Should the worker proceed when the client gives permission, even though the social worker knows that the client's consent is less than informed?

b. Voluntariness. Consent is meaningful only when it is given freely. But many social workers practice in a setting where the client has no or little freedom. Prisoners and committed mental patients are the classic examples of nonvoluntary clients, but there are many others in situations where their consent must also be considered less than voluntary. In the *Kaimowitz* decision (42 USLA 2063, 1973) the court ruled that persons whose privileges and eventual discharge depend on their cooperating with the custodial staff cannot give legally adequate voluntary consent. It may be asked how a social worker can practice in a setting where, by definition, consent will not be voluntary. At the very least, these social workers will almost constantly face serious ethical dilemmas. The usual practice of giving as much choice as possible under the circumstances may be the only feasible alternative, but this does not completely resolve the ethical dilemma facing the social worker practicing in such involuntary settings.

Consent also may be less than voluntary in settings which are usually classified as voluntary. Halleck (1971) questioned whether the wide array of pressures operating on both client and worker made truly voluntary consent possible even in private practice. And how voluntary will be the consent when the client believes it important to gain the worker's good will? The destitute single parent mother may agree with whatever her social worker suggests because she wants to qualify for assistance. The man who desperately wants a reconciliation with his estranged wife may agree with everything the social worker mentions because he believes that this is the way he can salvage his marriage. Even though these people came voluntarily to the social work agency, can their consent be considered voluntary? The dilemma facing these social workers centers around the area of client trust in the worker. Research has shown that trust or faith in the professional is a key component in effecting change. Yet frequently faith or trust results in a surrender of decision-making participation. Instead of voluntary consent, the client who has "blind faith" will agree with everything the professional says. The problem facing social workers is to develop and encourage trust, yet at the same time strengthen voluntary consent.

The problem of voluntary consent takes on special significance when a client wants to harm himself or herself, either by wishing to commit suicide or by wanting to engage in other self-destructive behavior. There are those who have argued that social workers have no right to interfere with persons who really want to harm themselves. Every person has a right to make this decision. Others have suggested that intervention, at least temporary intervention, may be justified in order to determine whether the contemplated action is fully voluntary. Gewirth (1978:264), contending that "the conditions of voluntary consent are never fulfilled in such cases (since) only abysmal ignorance or deep emotional trauma can lead persons to extreme measures like these," would probably hold that a social worker has the obligation to intervene in order to protect such persons' welfare.

    c. Competence. Informed consent presupposes that the person who gives consent is competent to do so. But many social work clients are less than fully competent. Young children, senile persons, and many retarded are generally considered less than competent to give informed consent to all or some decisions. While there is no agreement how old a child must be before it is considered competent, everyone agrees that an infant is never competent. The ethical dilemma arising out of questions of competence especially faces social workers engaged in such activities as adoption, foster placement, custody, abortion, contraception, and euthanasia. To the extent that children are involved in these situations (and often these are very young children), the social worker's dilemma becomes a difficult one.

The situation is not very different when working with older adults. How senile must a person be before a social worker can ethically ignore the oldster's wishes? And what are acceptable indicators of senility? Michael Heinrich (exemplar 3.10) may be old and give some indications of senile behavior, but does his renewed interest in sex with a much younger partner prove that he is no longer competent, as his children contend?

3.10:   Michael Heinrich's girlfriend

Michael Heinrich, seventy-seven years old, has been living alone since his wife died four years ago. Some months ago Heinrich became seriously ill. His married son and daughter arranged for round-the-clock nursing care in his apartment. One of these nurses, forty-year-old Lisa Nunn, has now become Heinrich's girlfriend. She has moved into the apartment and is telling everyone that she and Michael will be married next month. Heinrich's children are very upset by their father's behavior. They consider him senile. They have engaged an attorney to have their father declared incompetent. They have also arranged to have their father admitted to a retirement home. They told the home's social worker not to pay any attention to their father's rambling since he was obviously senile and no longer knew what was good for him. They indicated that their father's sexual phantasies about his "girlfriend" were only one indication that he is senile and no longer competent to make decisions.

When visiting Mr. Heinrich for the preadmission interview, the social worker was able to speak with him only in the presence of Ms. Nunn. Heinrich gave the appearance of being very old and participated only rarely in the conversation. But he stated clearly that he did not want to leave his apartment and his girlfriend.

The dilemma of informed consent takes on special significance when the client is not an individual, but a community, a neighborhood, or a large collectivity. A social worker involved in a neighborhood renewal program must consider whether the official decision makers really represent all residents. Does the informed consent of representatives suffice or must every resident consent? What is the situation when the initiative for intervention comes from outside of the collectivity? It will not be possible to obtain informed consent if the social worker's first objective is to raise the group's consciousness to the fact that there is a problem. Requiring every member's consent may be tantamount to ruling out any intervention activity, yet entering the situation without informed consent is a violation of the professional ethics. What should a social worker do in these and similar circumstances?

Ways of Consenting. Oliver Goldsmith (1764) wrote that "Silence gives consent," but social workers have learned that silence, as well as nonverbal signs, such as nods, or even the verbal "yes," may be deceptive and may indicate something other than consent. Clients may be ashamed to withhold consent or simply not understand with what they have been asked to agree. Though we noted earlier that clients often do not seem to listen, the social worker is still obligated to offer a full explanation of what will be involved in the intervention, what the projected benefits and risks are, what other options are available and what might happen if the client does not consent. And all this must be presented in language and concepts that the client can understand.

It has been suggested that good clinical practice will resolve all of the dilemmas arising around informed consent. If a client is involved in decision-making, questions of consent will not arise. Yet even formal contracting will not resolve all the problems involved in obtaining informed consent. The power gap between client and worker does not always permit contract negotiations between equals. Some coercion may be brought into play and this may force the client to agree to a contract which is not entirely of her or his choosing. The routine use of written consent forms has led to much abuse because often clients do not really understand what they are signing. Many of the forms used by social agencies are either very difficult to read and understand or are so general that they become practically meaningless. One writer concluded that "there is good reason to believe that many, perhaps most, who sign the forms are displaying trust more than understanding when they pen their signatures to the forms" (*Los Angeles Times*, June 8, 1980, p. 1). NASW's Policy on Information Utilization and Confidentiality (1975) does not spell out the criteria for informed consent. The

American Red Cross has addressed this issue by insisting that "before the 'Release of Confidential Information' form is signed, the service-to-military families worker must be assured that the client or responsible representative understands what information is to be given, to whom, and for what purpose" (ARC 2049, October 1974). The problem may be that many of the forms used today were designed primarily to protect agency and workers from possible malpractice suits rather than to guarantee informed consent. The challenge is to develop a form which is both readable and sufficiently specific, but which does not scare the client by focusing only on the harmful consequences.

DILEMMA 5

Sharing Limited Resources

The value of equity states that every person has an equal right to social benefits and social burdens (Rawls 1971:302, Frankena 1973:49). From the societal value of equity social work has derived the professional ethic that all clients have a right to an equal share of the available resources. Yet this ethic may create conflict for the social worker who is committed to meet the specific needs of each client. For example, a social worker in a family agency may be scheduled for client interviews thirty hours a week. Is each of this worker's thirty clients entitled to one hour per week? What about Peter Barr, a client who is currently facing a major family crisis and who this week needs many hours of counseling? His social worker can devote this additional time to Barr only by allotting less time to other clients. Is such an unequal use of time ethically permissible?

Time is a very limited and precious resource in the social work process. Many strategies are ruled out simply because staff time is not available to implement them. Social workers know that there are times clients could receive more effective service if only there were time available to provide the service. The need to observe equity in the allocation of time creates various ethical dilemmas, one of which is illustrated by the interview with Donna Schild (exemplar 3.11).

3.11:   Incest in the Schild family

Donna Schild is a cute looking thirteen year old with a history of truancy, alcoholism, drug experimentation, and several attempts at running away from home. Her parents appear warm and accepting, but the family agency worker who has been meeting weekly with Donna for the past four weeks suspects that the real problem is Donna's home.

Today was the fifth session with Donna. The conversation was routine and little of significance was said until three minutes before the next client was scheduled. Donna suddenly opened up and started to relate some very significant and emotionally charged material. Both her father and her older brother have tried to have sexual relations with her repeatedly, but thus far she has not let them go all the way. When she told her mother about this, her mother told her to forget that this ever happened. As Donna related this material she became noticeably more excited.

The social worker realized that the interview could not be terminated just because time was up. But how long could the next client be kept waiting? Donna could easily use another hour of time. But that would not be fair to the other clients scheduled for this day. Furthermore, if Donna was not exaggerating, there would be need to make immediate arrangements to remove her from her home. This might take many additional hours of the worker's time, hours which were scheduled for other urgent assignments. What should the worker do?

What would you do? What other ethical dilemmas does this worker face in addition to the equity dilemma? What are the worker's obligations to Donna's parents? To the community?

Consider the problem facing the social workers of Centro Hispano, a Red Feather agency in Westport, a community which has always had a large concentration of Spanish-speaking immigrants. Centro Hispano was started as an indigenous self-help group by immigrants from Latin America in the 1960s. Nowadays its budget is met largely by the Community Chest, supplemented at times by specific Federal grants. Though volunteers are still utilized, most assignments are handled by professional staff members, but decision-making powers are vested in the agency's board of directors, made up largely of veteran Spanish-speaking residents of the community.

3.12: Cuban refugees in Westport

Early last year more than 400 new Cuban refugee families arrived in Westport. Centro Hispano was able to generate a special one-time $100,000 grant to help in their adjustment process. The board of directors decided after a lengthy discussion to allocate 20 percent of this grant to employ two more part-time social workers and to distribute the remaining funds directly to the refugee families to help them in their adjustment. The detailed rules for distributing these funds were to be developed by the agency's staff.

The next staff meeting was devoted to developing criteria for distributing the funds. The agency's director, Sandra Lopez, argued that equity demanded that each of the refugee families receive an equal cash grant of approximately $175 which each family could use as it wanted. Several staff members agreed with Ms. Lopez. But another staff group, led by social worker Blanca Borrayo, urged that the limited funds be used where they could do the most good. Since the basic needs of the refugee families were already met by the local and Federal governments, these new monies should be saved for special needs where an intensive use of resources could best achieve the the desired objective. Each staff group believed that its proposal was most in line with professional ethics.

If you had been participating as a staff member in this staff meeting, how would you have voted? Why?

A special aspect of this dilemma arises out of the focused professional relationship (see also Section 8 in this chapter). The worker may feel an obligation to provide follow-up services to the person or group whose life has been changed, yet other social work values counterindicate a prolonged dependency relationship. Even when a long-term supportive relationship might be indicated, the needs of other clients and agency policy might not make this possible. The growing popularity of time-limited help is, in part, an administrative response to the social work ethic of sharing limited resources equally. What criteria can a social worker utilize to resolve the dilemma of providing services above and beyond what the employing agency has authorized?

DILEMMA 6

Priority of Client's Interests/Worker's Interests

Giving priority to the client's interests is one of the cornerstones of every professional code of ethics from antiquity until our own days. Since the client generally cannot control the professional's activities, this ethic is meant to safeguard the client from exploitation. Perhaps the best-known violation of this ethical principle involves unnecessary surgery, but in fact members of every profession have at one time or another ignored this principle by placing their own self-interest ahead of that of their clients. Recently it was charged that some teachers have failed students in order to assure a full classroom in the face of dwindling school populations and threatened teacher cutbacks (*Time*, June 16, 1980). This charge is no different than earlier charges that some institutional social workers had failed to recommend the discharge of institutionalized children in order to assure continued state supplementation and thus their own continued employment.

The reader might wonder how this ethical principle can create a dilemma for the vast majority of contemporary social workers who are salaried employees of social agencies, most of whom have more clients than they can serve. These social workers receive their biweekly salary check regardless of what they do. Nor is it to their economic advantage to ignore this ethic. Perhaps an occasional social worker in private practice may be tempted to place financial gain above client's interest, but employed social workers simply do not face this dilemma.

Yet this dilemma touches every social worker when the issue is self-preservation and survival, rather than financial gain. Must a social worker give priority to a client's interest even when this may result in the worker's death? Or in severe harm to the worker's children? Or do considerations of self-preservation and survival legitimize actions which ordinarily would be considered unethical? Must Russell Becker (exemplar 1.3) endanger his life in order to serve the interests of Alice Andrew who has been abused by her father? Or is there justification for Becker to withdraw from the case? Must social workers at all times serve their clients' interests, regardless of the consequences? Or can they ethically declare that under certain unusual circumstances the professional obligation to serve their clients' interests is no longer primary?

Gewirth's Principle of Generic Consistency (1978:135) may be helpful in considering this dilemma. He stated, "Act in accord with the generic rights of your recipients (i.e., your clients) *as well as of yourself*" (emphasis added). Gewirth evidently suggests that there is no need for the worker to abdicate his own rights, especially when these conflict with another's rights. Gewirth's principle was not developed to guide professional actions and there are those who will argue that it does not apply to professionals who should always be guided by the ethic of giving priority to the client's interests, no matter what the consequences. Those who would follow Gewirth's lead must consider the question of whether ethics are relative? Do ethical obligations change according to the consequences? And what must be the degree of potential harm to relax the ethical priorities due to clients?

DILEMMA 7

Choice of Effective Interventive Methods

In many ways the interventive methods which social workers choose create ethical problems. Our society places great emphasis upon pragmatism and technology. It constantly emphasizes efficiency and effectiveness with little attention paid to ethical questions. Many social workers have been influenced by these attitudes and believe that interventive methods are value free and present no ethical problems. But the choice of interventive methods does have ethical implications and may lead to ethical problems. Social workers who are aware of this will in the ordinary course of events choose interventive methods which are ethical. Whenever this is not possible or difficult, serious ethical dilemmas occur. One source for this dilemma is that social workers are typically employed by organizations. Often this leads to ethical conflicts about the choice of methods since their choice or availability may be limited by the organization, as Olga Casio (exemplar 3.13) discovered.

3.13: Olga Casio and her supervisor

Olga Casio is a school social worker in an elementary school in a working class neighborhood. Serena Martorana is a nine-year-old girl who misbehaves in the classroom. She is a foster child and evidently deeply in need of acceptance. Some classmates view her as a nice girl but others see her as being "different."

In this school, difficult children are referred to the social worker as a matter of course, because "teachers do not have time to work with each problem child." Upon exploring this case, Ms. Casio thought that the teacher contributed to the problem of scapegoating Serena. She thought there was need for work with the teacher and the principal in order to help this child. However, her supervisor rejected this strategy pointing out that in this school system the social worker's job is to relieve the teachers by working with the children and their parents, not to change the teachers.

Ms. Casio is in a quandary. How should she proceed? Should she offer Serena casework even though she knows this will not serve to help the child? What responsibility does she have for attempting to change policy and how should she go about it?

Many social workers believe that insight therapy is the most sophisticated and valued form of professional help. Because of this peer pressure many social workers provide insight therapy even in situations where other forms of help may be more appropriate.

3.14:   Mr. Biao's depression

Harry Biao is a seventy-five-year-old Chinese-American who arrived in this country fifty-three years ago. Until recently, he owned a hardware store in Chinatown. His wife died ten years ago and he now lives by himself. The social service home-maker, Mrs. Hua, reported that Mr. Biao appeared depressed and almost never left his apartment and was uncommunicative whether she spoke to him in English or Cantonese.

The problem of Mr. Biao was presented at a staff meeting. Mr. Biao's worker argued for involving him in the Chinese Community Center's program for the aged. Other workers suggested that it would be best to provide therapy which would give Mr. Biao insight into his problems. This has been the agency's customary way of handling problems.

The pressure on Mr. Biao's worker did not come from agency directives or supervisor, but from the peer group. We know from experimental research and from life situations that peer group pressure can be even stronger than organizational rules so that the ethical dilemma around choice of interventive methods is a very real one.

Ethical choices also must be made in situations in which the social worker may have expertise in one or several types of intervention methods, but another method in which the worker is less expert appears to be indicated.

3.15:   No other family therapist

The Martin family has been experiencing difficulties between the parents and the two adolescent children. There has been a series of conflicts in which everyone involved has been shouting at each other, calling each other names, or in some cases not talking to each other for several days. Ms. Martin, the mother, has come to Ms. Aberdeen, a private social worker for help with her feelings of failing as a mother. After talking with Ms. Martin, Ms. Aberdeen feels that the problem goes beyond Ms. Martin, and that family therapy is indicated. Even though she is a competent caseworker, she has had no experience in providing family therapy. But in this rural county, there is only one family therapist. Unfortunately, Ms. Aberdeen questions the competence of this person.

Should Ms. Aberdeen provide family therapy, knowing that she lacks expertise in this or should she offer a second choice method (individual treatment) which she does well? Or, should she refer this case to a therapist about whom she has serious questions?

DILEMMA 8

Limited Nature of the Professional Relationship

The professional helping relationship, by definition, is one which focusses on a specific area of personal behavior or environment for which help is sought. This is a limited relationship in contrast to the broad primary-type relationship which most people treasure. Clients often misunderstand the friendliness and informality which characterize their contact with a social worker because they are used to a high degree of formality, impersonality, and even indifference from other professionals. Here we will not discuss the practice problems which arise out of this misunderstanding, but focus instead on the ethical problems which face social workers because of their commitment to the ethical application of the professional relationship. The major ethical dilemma in this area occurs when a social worker believes that the solution of a client's problem requires more than what the traditional definition of the limited professional relationship permits.

Anomie is a major problem in the contemporary world. People have become rootless and many have lost the connection with their sources and their fellow human beings. Many symptoms reflect this anomie. Workers soon realize that treating the symptoms without resolving the core problem is often not sufficient. One of the objectives in the treatment of this type of problem is the establishment or reestablishment of more meaningful interpersonal relationships. Should not social workers provide a model of the desirable interpersonal relationship? How can a client learn a new interaction pattern if the limited professional relationship does not permit the social worker to model and demonstrate?

Some social workers hide behind the limited professional relationship because they are uncomfortable with their clients' lifestyle and culture. But many more social workers want to express empathy with their clients. Without wanting to imitate a lifestyle that is not authentic for them, they want to learn and participate in the life of their clients, since they cannot be helpful if they do not have this knowledge. But such relationships cannot be limited to the 9:00 A.M. to 5:00 P.M., Monday through Friday work week. However, is it ethical for a social worker to accept a Sunday dinner invitation from a client? Or to join a client at the local bar on Friday evening? May a worker reciprocate and invite a client for supper at home or in a restaurant? Practice wisdom has given a fairly clear and generally negative answer to all of these questions, but increasingly social workers express discomfort with this iron curtain that has been erected between them and their clients.

The NASW Code of Ethics specifically addresses only one aspect of this dilemma. It prohibits all sexual activities with clients (section II F 5). Some social workers have questioned this ethic, pointing out that nowadays a large number of the problems brought to the attention of social workers involve problems of sexual dysfunction (Schúltz 1975). Professional intervention might include techniques which were unthinkable only a few decades ago, including therapeutic infidelity, masturbation, and therapeutic sexual intercourse between client and social worker or surrogate. The exemplar of Jill Jordan (3.16) illustrates why some social workers feel that the traditional interpretation of the professional relationship may be too limiting.

3.16:   Jill Jordan's inferiority complex

Jill Jordan, a thirty-five-year-old divorcee, started social work treatment with the complaint that she had been unable to obtain sexual fulfillment with two husbands and a series of boyfriends. In fact, she reported that she never had satisfactory sex. Both of her ex-husbands told her that she was an inadequate partner and left her because of this. A succession of boyfriends left her for the same reason. By now she has developed a severe inferiority complex about herself as a woman and as a sexual partner. She is wondering whether she may have lesbian tendencies which prevent her from enjoying sex with men.

Bob Temple, an experienced social worker, was assigned as her therapist. During the course of treatment Temple was very understanding and warmly responsive to Jordan. His objective was to restore Jill's faith in herself. But progress was extremely slow and difficult because of continuing unsuccessful relationships with men even while she was in treatment.

Temple thought that progress might be faster if he could help Jill regain her sense of worth as a woman. One of his techniques involved much touching. Jill responded positively to this. After several months Temple thought that it might be clinically appropriate to have full sexual relations with Jill so that she could become aware of her capacity for achieving sexual satisfaction.

Here we want to analyze the ethical aspects of this clinical decision. Is Temple proposing an honest relationship or is he engaging in sex under false pretenses? What other options should Temple have explored with Jill Jordan? Do these other options present the same ethical dilemmas? What if the social worker had been a woman who had used herself to help Jill enjoy sexual relations with other women?

DILEMMA 9

Suspension of Judgment

Social workers are expected to suspend judgment about the behavior and actions of individuals even when their own values or societal values clearly demand a judgment. Suspension of judgment is a basic expectation of the social work profession. Yet the social work practitioner encounters many obstacles when trying to apply this ethic since every decision involves the application of judgment, if not the social worker's judgment, then that of someone else.

When a social worker helps one group to attain the satisfaction of its legitimate needs, another group with equally legitimate needs may be harmed. A worker's intervention may result in a redistribution of resources and funds, changing long-standing institutional arrangements. As a result, one group may have its deficiencies reduced, while another may be further weakened. On what basis does a social worker support one group and not another? Is this assessment made on the basis of the social worker's judgment? That of the group requesting help? The community? What weight should the social worker give to competing values? Should the social worker adjudicate among conflicting claims, all of which may be legitimate and worthy? Or, shall the law of the jungle prevail?

The emerging multicultural ethos of our society has created new ethical dilemmas for social workers. Having abandoned the "melting pot" approach, social workers now believe that every ethnic and cultural group must be encouraged and helped to maintain itself as a distinct group. But what should be the social worker's stance when a given behavioral feature associated with an ethnic or cultural group makes it difficult for a specific client to obtain a job or health care? Or, what should social workers do when the satisfaction of the needs of a person from one group means that the needs of a person from another group will only be met partially?

Do social workers have a responsibility to examine the ethical nature and quality of the problems which people bring to them? Or are they technicians who help regardless of the moral aspects of the situation? The following exemplar raises questions of this type in a relatively noncharged setting.

3.17:   A smoking lounge for high school students

Kate Collins is a school social worker. She is a member of the student-faculty council which recommends policy in the local high school. At a recent meeting several student members proposed setting up a "smoking lounge" to eliminate the safety hazard of students' smoking illegally in the bathrooms and locker rooms.

Kate Collins is convinced, on the basis of her reading of many research reports, that smoking is very dangerous to one's health. She believes that nothing should be done that might encourage young people to smoke. How can she be a party to a recommendation which she considers potentially injurious?

Some will think that smoking, although injurious, is not to be considered immoral, yet think that suicide is indeed immoral. What would a social worker who believes that suicide is immoral do if the social agency assigned him or her to a staff committee responsible for preparing a guide for committing suicide? Would it make an ethical difference if the distribution of this pamphlet were limited to persons with terminal illnesses?

Society, with near unanimity, condemns incest. Yet the incidence of incestual relationships that comes to the attention of social workers seems to be on the rise. This statistical rise may be due to the fact that people feel freer to talk about all types of sexual activities, including incest, although there may be an actual increase in the incidence of incest. The ethical question facing a social worker who receives such information is how to react to it. Does the social worker don a value-free mask and listen to a report of an incident of incestual behavior with the same equanimity as he would to any other problem behavior? Or must the worker communicate the cultural disvalues that the community sees in incest. A possible change in community values which may have radical implications for professional practice may be indicated by the following citation quoted by a nationally syndicated columnist (George G. Will, *Boston Globe*, May 26, 1980, citing James Ramey):

> Many girls are in the truest sense of the word their fathers' lovers. Many have the same type of relationship that adults have, and some resent community intervention and are difficult to work with, particularly when professionals carry over a cultural bias that incest is wrong. . . .

Does it make a difference whether father or daughter or both are clients of the social worker? Does the age of the girl matter? Are there cultural factors which might make a difference in the ethical implications of incestuous behavior? What if the clients' ethnic group does not proscribe father-daughter relations which do not involve penetration?

The three behaviors discussed above—smoking, suicide, and incest—form a matrix of ethical intensity. They suggest that beyond a certain point almost every social worker will abandon the value-free stance suggested by the ethic of suspension of judgment. But the ethical dilemma is more serious than these "unusual" examples suggest because it occurs at every step in the social work process. The social worker who "suspends judgment" when a client relates a promiscuous episode or an aggressive behavior incident at work is as judgmental as the colleague who indicates disapproval. When a client feels guilty about the behavior and the worker does not react to the description of this behavior, the client may interpret the worker's silence as approval of this behavior. The real ethical dilemma facing social workers, then, is that suspension of judgment is not possible. Some have tried to avoid this dilemma by suggesting to a client that they disapprove of the specific behavior, but not of the client. This is a fine, almost legalistic distinction which may seem to solve the ethical problem, but creates other practice problems.

MAKING CHOICES AND ACCEPTING RESPONSIBILITY

Social workers must accept responsibility for what they do. They are accountable to their clients, to their agency, to their profession, to society, and to themselves. They cannot hide behind the Nuremberg argument that they had no control over their activities. It just is not acceptable to claim that "I couldn't help it" or "I was forced to do it." Making responsible choices on the basis of one's best professional judgment is a crucial imperative for social work practitioners.

It may be more comfortable to leave choices to events as they develop, but few responsible social workers would do so. However, many social workers have suggested that all decisions and choices should be made by clients, not social workers. This suggestion may exemplify professional practice ideals, but it does not avoid all ethical problems. When there is more than one client, the social worker still needs to make judgments about whose decision to give priority attention. And even when there is only one client, decisions about what information to provide must still be made. Should confidential information, for example, be supplied when this knowledge is essential for competent consent or client decision-making?

The essence of professionalism is making responsible choices and accepting responsibility for these. Formal agency and informal peer accountability systems are helpful, but ultimately the responsibility for making ethical decisions must be that of every social worker.

EXERCISES

1. Take a case with which you are familiar (or take one of the exemplars from Appendix A) and analyze it as follows:
    a. Identify the participants according to the scheme proposed in the boxed-in model, earlier in this chapter.
    b. Indicate the different expectations which the participants might have of the social worker (role-set conflict).
    c. In addition, indicate the role conflict that you (or the social worker in the exemplar) might experience because you occupy different roles.
2. Imagine that you are an agency director and have just become aware that your agency manual makes no reference to the subject of informed consent. There have been several incidents in the past few months that indicate that some staff members do violence to this principle. Prepare a two-to-three-paragraph section on *informed consent* for the manual. Be sure that you make it sufficiently specific so that it can guide the efforts of all agency workers.
3. Role play with fellow staff members, a spouse, friend, or classmate, the meeting of the Centro Hispano staff (exemplar 3.12).
4. The 1979 NASW Code of Ethics specifically prohibits social workers from engaging in sexual activities with their clients. Some social workers have argued that there is no scientific evidence that

such activity is harmful and this ethic is no longer appropriate in a society which permits a wide variety of lifestyles. Present arguments both for changing and keeping this ethic.

5. Consider Callahan's comment (1980:1228) that "only rarely can ethical analysis and prescription lead the way in social and cultural change." Does this observation hold for social work? If so, how can social workers meet their role as change agents and yet conduct themselves ethically?

6. Two adult clients, a brother and a sister, have been living together and have regularly engaged in incestuous relations since they graduated from college. They have come to the social agency to make arrangements for their aged mother. In the course of your contact with them they freely discuss their living arrangements and their preferred lifestyle. Examine the NASW Code of Ethics to see if it provides you with guidance on how you should act in this situation.

4 Ethical Decision-Making

Social workers constantly make ethical choices. A client tells her social worker that she is planning to commit suicide. A group member asks his social worker to lie so that he can get a job after he has been unemployed for nine months. A client tells her worker that she has been embezzling funds from a business to pay for her son's open heart surgery. A young man threatens to harm a fellow worker who has raped his fiancee. Each of these situations, like those discussed in the previous chapter, confront the social worker with one or more ethical dilemmas because they involve conflicting ethical obligations.

CHARACTERISTICS OF DECISION-MAKING

In this chapter we will discuss the philosophical and practical background for ethical decision-making which leads to ethical professional activity. Making decisions is seldom a split-second act, but typically is a process or series of thoughts and actions which occur over time and which lead a person to act (or not to act) in a particular manner. Every decision is approached step by step, so that one moves gradually through a series of stages in considering the question until one reaches the end of the process, the decision itself. But other persons react, facts change, the situation is altered by the decision and by other changes in the environment even after a "final" decision has been made, so that the decision-making process

63

should continue to deal with the flow of new information and newly emerging conditions.

In real life it is most difficult to isolate *one* discrete decision. Decision-making, in one sense, is like an ever-continuing network or decision-tree. Choices are influenced by previous decisions, in turn lead to various new directions, and continue on the following branches and pathways. For the purpose of improving the social worker's skill in ethical decision-making and for helping social workers understand what is involved in ethical decisions, a model of decision-making is desirable. Such a model will simplify the realities of life by focusing on only one specific decision. A model is a permissible didactic device as long as social workers understand that in real life every decision is preceded and followed by other decisions, many of which will have a direct bearing on the professional matter under consideration. Again, the purpose of a model is to simplify reality in order to help us understand better what happens in the real world.

The decision-making process can occur within seconds or take place over a long period of time. Either way, our decision-making model includes the following elements:

1. Identification of the problem or question which requires a decision.
2. Establishing goals or objectives.
3. Identifying alternative targets and strategies.
4. Assessing and weighing possible outcomes of each option in terms of goal achievement.
5. Selecting the best or most correct option.
6. Implementing the option selected.
7. Evaluating the results of the decision and action.

This decision-making model is a general model and is not limited to ethical decisions. When the focus is on ethical decisions, the ethical aspect becomes part and parcel of every element. This model is based on the assumption that social workers can rationally plan what is needed in order to intervene in human situations. Social workers place much emphasis on the "conscious use of self," on being aware of one's self and others, and on making decisions and taking action only after careful deliberation in order to minimize the possibility of irrational, impulsive, and unplanned consequences.

Before illustrating the decision-making process through an exemplar, we must point out several additional features which impinge on ethical decision-making. As already noted in the previous chapters, social workers must often act without access to complete information about situations and about all of the potential consequences of their actions or lack of actions. This lack of information limits, but does not invalidate the rational decision-making model. Further, the decision-making process does not follow a straight, linear process. There will be a constant going back and forth between the various decision-making stages outlined above. For example, as some options are assessed, additional options may be identified. When difficulties are encountered in the implementation stage, there may be need to return to the identification stage to gather more information. Finally, it is important to recognize that values influence all elements of the ethical decision-making process and are inseparable from other components of the process.

Let us now analyze a case example and consider how ethical dilemmas arise in the decision-making process. The names and details may differ, but the ethical dilemmas are similar to those faced by social workers in almost every practice setting.

4.1: Debbie Roberts is pregnant

Debbie Roberts, a twelve-year-old sixth-grader, is ten weeks pregnant. She has been a good student and was never before in trouble at school. She had never seen the school social worker and was sent to the worker by the school nurse now only because she refused to talk to the nurse about her condition.

In her conversation with Debbie, the social worker learned that Debbie did not want an abortion, but wanted the social worker's help to make arrangements so that she could carry to full term, without her parents knowing that she was pregnant.

We shall approach the analysis of this exemplar, like others in this book, with a primary focus on the worker. The facts are fairly clear, but ethical dilemmas occur already around the second phase, establishing objectives. The social worker must weigh the following considerations, each of which presents an ethical dilemma:

1. The worker's professional experience suggests that Debbie's request is not realistic. A twelve-year-old girl cannot carry to full-term without her parents knowing about it. Good professional practice would suggest that the worker help Debbie understand this and help her discuss this situation with her parents. But since time is of the essence for a "safe" abortion, there may not be sufficient time to follow this strategy. Is an emergency intervention which ignores the client's wishes justified?

2. Pregnancy for a twelve year old may cause damage to her emotional and physical development, as well as place serious barriers in the way of her achieving social, educational, and life goals. Does this justify ignoring Debbie's wishes?

3. Is a twelve-year-old girl competent to decide whether or not to have a child? Does Debbie give evidence of being sufficiently mature to make this kind of a decision? Would the worker raise the same questions if Debbie had requested help in arranging for an abortion?

4. Can and should the worker impose a decision on this client? Should she persuade Debbie to have an abortion?

Upon what basis can Debbie's social worker resolve the ethical dilemmas posed by this exemplar? Parenthetically, we must note again that the concept "ethical dilemma" and "ethical problem" is not entirely accurate. We are really talking here and elsewhere about the ethical aspects of practice problems. What are the ethical considerations that Debbie's social worker must keep in mind as she makes practice decisions?

Ethical decision-making does not involve the automatic application of arbitrary rules. If that were the case, there would be few ethical problems. Usually, the social worker does not face a simple choice between a good option and a bad option. Instead there are various choices, each one of which contains both positive and negative features, as was true in the choices facing Debbie's worker. In such a situation the skilled worker will assess and weigh all possible strategies and outcomes and then select the option which appears to be the most ethical one.

SOURCES FOR ETHICAL DECISION-MAKING

Ethical decisions are neither idiosyncratic, nor are they created out of thin air. Deeply rooted in societal values, they deal with what is considered right and what is considered wrong. Here we will consider four major sources from which professional social workers can derive ethical decisions:

1. Philosophical values.
2. Professional code of ethics.
3. Practice wisdom.
4. Awareness and personal professional experience.

We shall examine each of these sources in the following pages.

Philosophical Values

Philosophy is the discipline which has devoted most time and energy to the study of ethics and to an inquiry into the nature of right and wrong actions, as well as to questions concerning ultimate goals. Philosophers have organized ethics into three major areas:

1. *Descriptive* ethics seek to describe moral and ethical experiences.

2. *Normative* ethics seek to arrive at a set of acceptable judgments regarding moral obligations, moral values, and nonmoral values. They aim at determining what ought to be, both on the individual and the societal level. Normative ethics are concerned not only with the individual, but examine such societal issues as the distribution of wealth, the place of violence in human affairs, and questions of war and peace.

3. *Critical* or meta-ethics attempt to explain the theoretical meaning and justification of judgments about obligations and values. Since this third area has few direct implications for professional ethical decision-making, we will limit our considerations to the first two areas.

Philosophers have followed two different approaches to the field of ethics and ethical decision-making. Some follow *teleological* theories and others, *deontological* theories.

1. Those who justify ethical decisions in terms of their consequences are known as *teleologists*. These philosophers state that a given course of action should be chosen not because it is inherently good, but because it leads to desired results. The amount of good which is produced, or the balance of good over evil, and not any absolute standard, should serve as a criterion for reaching a decision. Teleological theories differ with respect to the intended beneficiary of the action. Ethical egoism states that one should always maximize one's own good; that is, one should endeavor to do what is best for oneself, never mind the consequences for others. Ethical utilitarians, on the other hand, suggest that the greatest good for the greatest number of persons is what counts.

2. Others hold that actions are inherently right or wrong, apart from any consequences to which they may lead. These philosophers, known as *deontologists*, hold, for example, that altruism is inherently good, even though a decision based on altruism may impoverish the decision-maker. Most, but not all deontologists hold that ethical rules can be formulated and that these rules should hold under all circumstances. Thus, they would suggest that the rule, "A social worker shall never lie to a client," is correct and applies at all times, no matter how much damage may be created by the social worker's telling the truth.

Kant was the first of modern philosophers to make deontological concepts central in an ethical system. He taught in a clear and uncompromising way that categorical imperatives were unconditional demands which were morally necessary and obligatory under all circumstances. An example of how social worker D who uses a deontological approach might reach a different decision than a colleague, social worker T, who bases decisions on teleological principles, was suggested by Reamer (1979:235). In this example, the social worker has discovered that a public assistance client has failed to report some part-time income. The problem is how the social worker should respond to this discovery. Worker D argues that it is inherently wrong to terminate aid for a needy recipient. Since reporting income will result in termination of assistance, worker D may overlook this instance of rule-violation. Worker T, on the other hand, might justify a temporary termination of benefits on the grounds that other recipients will learn from this example and will in the future report all income, thus leading to the generally desirable result of a reduction in the cost of welfare, which in turn might permit a lowering of taxes, an outcome from which many people will benefit. However, neither worker D nor worker T will avoid facing other ethical dilemmas because the arguments cited address only one aspect of the situation. For worker D there remains the categorical imperative of observing the law, which demands that every rule violation be reported. The effect of cutting off aid must be considered by worker T. What will be the social and emotional costs to the recipient's family, costs which society must pay sooner or later? Do short-term gains offset long-term costs?

In the example cited each of the workers is faced by two or more rules. Each of these rules suggests a different strategy. This makes for the ethical problem. Socrates was the first philosopher to become aware of this dilemma. He tried to develop criteria which would guide persons in determining which of two rules should take precedence, but evidently he was no more successful than the other philosophers who have wrestled with this problem in the thousands of years since his day.

Professional Code of Ethics

One of the hallmarks of professions is their development of codes of ethics. As we have seen earlier, the social work profession has over time evolved a code of ethics which has been revised and rewritten as the profession, society, and the needs of people have changed. Professional codes assist social workers to conduct their professional lives and to make ethical decisions on the basis of expert opinion and a reasonable consensus in the profession. Nevertheless, social workers often find it difficult to decide upon ethical issues, even though the code is a major source of reference for such decisions.

The professional code of ethics is an attempt to shift ethical problems from the realm of individual dilemmas to group decisions. As such it is an intermediate step because many of the big ethical problems can no longer be handled and decided by individual practitioners, even when backed by a code of ethics. The most bothersome and difficult ethical problems need societal decisions.

Thus the development of a more just system of distributing resources in the face of chronic and continuing poverty presents ethical problems far more complex than those which an individual worker, or even a professional association, is competent to handle.

Practice Wisdom

The NASW Code of Ethics is a formal statement, outlining the ethically desirable behavior expected of social workers. This formal code is supplemented by a more informal practice wisdom which guides the daily activities of social workers. Practice wisdom is developed in collegial interactions and in discussions about specific case situations, while the formal code provides more general guidelines. For example, the social worker who discovered that a foster parent was molesting the foster child, but who knows that the social agency will not back a worker in bringing legal charges against foster parents, will not find specific advice in the code of ethics on how to deal with this situation. This worker will turn to practice wisdom for help.

Practice wisdom, because it tends to be idiosyncratic, can be contradictory and even wrong. For example, for many years it was held that children should always go with their mother when a family was split by divorce. Social workers generally followed this guide and arranged for children to go with their mother, no matter what the circumstances. More recently, practice wisdom has reflected the changes which have occurred in the larger society and social workers now follow other guidelines in custody disputes.

The choice of adoptive homes for Black children provides another example of how practice wisdom tends to follow value changes in the larger society. Initially, when discrimination was so prevalent in American society, Black children were placed only in Black homes. If no Black adoptive parents were available, there was just no alternative. As a result, in those days most Black children who could not remain in their own or in a relative's home were placed in institutions, even though social workers knew then that institutions were not the best places to raise children. Later, in the 1950s, when the goal of societal integration became paramount, social workers tried to find the best home for each child, no matter whether the skin color or ethnic background of child and adoptive parent matched. More recently, there has been another change in the advice given to social workers by practice wisdom. Increasingly Black children again are placed only with Black adoptive families. This is in line with the more recent societal emphasis on developing a pluralistic, multicultural and multiethnic society, where each ethnic and cultural group must be provided with an opportunity to continue its own development. Today, social workers try to find a Black home for each Black child in order to provide a relevant and meaningful ethnic upbringing, even if finding such homes takes longer and creates some temporary discomfort for the child. Both the earlier and the later advice was viewed as ethical, each in its time.

Awareness and Personal Professional Experience

Most social workers engage in ethical behavior most of the time. If this were not the case, the profession would be constantly besieged by complaints from clients, social work colleagues, and others. Ethical issues of importance, however, arise both in routine and in dramatic situations. Social workers become aware in varying degrees of the ethical dilemmas which arise out of their own and their colleagues' professional experiences. For example, social workers are not blind to the fact that confidential case records are read by many persons for various purposes, including data collection, accountability, and research; these records may also be read by other professionals who will be working with the same client or family members at some future date. The ethical dilemma facing social workers in this situation arises out of two professional obligations: (1) the client's right to confidentiality, and (2) the professional's need to record the social work process. The question is how to discharge both obligations ethically. Only when a worker is aware of the possible contradiction can the problem be addressed responsibly and ethically.

Generally, most social workers agree on what is right and ethical. However, at times a social worker must swim against the tide of conventional social work knowledge and practice. Social workers who challenge the community or the agency within which they work in order to provide better and more ethical service may risk ostracism and loss of job. Social workers who refuse to compromise their ethical stance on constitutional or other grounds also risk sanctions. These social workers base their professional actions on their own demand for ethical behavior at a time that others may be hedging or be unaware of the ethical implications of their activities.

ALERTNESS TO ETHICAL DILEMMAS

Social workers need to raise their consciousness about ethical dilemmas before they become the victims of situations which demand ethical decision-making and action. They must become sensitive to and perceptive about situations in which ethical questions and issues may occur. Is it unethical to raise or lower a test score in order to obtain a needed resource for a client? What if by doing so, one labels the client as mentally retarded or senile? What is the ethical responsibility of a social worker to a client who beats his wife? Does the ethic which obligates the giving of priority to a client's interests absolve the social worker from any obligation to the victim? Or is there another ethic which demands priority attention to a victim, no matter what the consequences for the client and no matter what the provocation?

Social workers need to train themselves to become aware and alert to ethical problems, even when this is counterindicated by the normal course of events. People, even professionals, try to avoid matters which will complicate their lives. But in the end such avoidance will lead only to greater complications.

Alertness to ethical problems is required not only of direct practitioners—social work supervisors, administrators, consultants, teachers, or members of Committees on Inquiry must also be alert to the ethical problems which directly or indirectly impinge on their activities. For example, what should be the response of a camp director who discovers that the camp buildings are used for illegal purposes during the winter, but who is told that his life will be in danger if he attempts to act upon this information? Is there an ethical problem here? What is it? How shall he assess the value of his own life as against the need of the poor children and senior adults who count on this camping experience? What obligations does he have for helping the police? Does it matter what type of illegal activity took place in camp?

EXAMINATION AND ASSESSMENT OF OPTIONS AND ALTERNATIVES

The social worker who is alert to ethical problems will examine and assess the available options and alternatives somewhat differently than a colleague who is not so concerned with the ethical aspect of practice. In this section we will review some of the considerations which are relevant to this phase of the decision-making process.

Efficiency and Effectiveness

The efficiency criterion is concerned with the relative costs (including funds, staff time, agency and community resources, and others) of achieving the stated objective. When one of two possible strategies, both of which will achieve the same results, requires less budget, less staff, or less time, it is said to be more efficient. The effectiveness criterion relates to the degree to which a proposed strategy results in achieving the desired outcome. When the use of one strategy results in halving the number of poor people, while another strategy reduces the poverty population by 80 percent, we say that the latter strategy is more effective. But in terms of the ethical aspects of social work practice, the efficiency and effectiveness criteria may not always be relevant or important. Killing poor people may be the most effective and most efficient way of reducing the poverty population, so long as no one asks what we are doing. Such a strategy is unethical and totally unacceptable, no matter how efficient or how effective.

We must also inquire whether a desirable goal justifies selecting an inefficient strategy. This question, the social work version of the traditional means-end argument, is particularly relevant in a time of shrinking welfare budgets. Do desirable ends justify any means, no matter how unacceptable these might be? For example, it has been said that in some states the deinstitutionalization of hospitalized mental patients was for the purpose of publicizing the need for community resources. This strategy of turning out of hospitals the mentally ill was adopted despite the fragility of many of the patients, despite the known lack of community resources, and despite the expressed intention of many of the state governments to reduce their welfare budgets, thus making it unlikely that community resources would be built in the reasonable future. Was it ethical to pursue a strategy which possibly could result in some long-range improvements, but at the cost of immediate damage to many people? Similar questions can be asked about Cloward and Piven's earlier strategy of overloading the welfare system in order to force a basic reform of that system; in this instance the system has not yet been reformed, but an increasing number of Americans have benefitted from this strategy. Was it ethical? Should we assess ethical choices differently when they result in success or partial success than when they end in failure?

Protection of Clients' Rights and Welfare

The definition of rights and privileges change over time. What is understood to be a right at one time may not be so defined at another and this may create ethical problems for social workers as well as other professionals. For example, journalists were once expected to get the news no matter what the obstacles. Today, however, there is great concern about the privacy rights of individuals and families; as a result journalists face an ethical dilemma—whether or not to pursue the news if it means disregarding a person's privacy. Similarly, health care was once viewed as a privilege. It was not considered a right, but a service which could be purchased by those who had the means. Yet today health care, particularly in emergency situations, is a right which is generally available to all, regardless of financial considerations.

Changing definitions of rights also create ethical problems for social workers. They are often involved in situations where it is not clear who the client is, or they may be involved in situations with two or more clients, each of whom deserves the protection of his or her rights. For example, to whom is a social worker in a genetics counseling service responsible? Who is the client? The woman who had come for assistance? Future generations? Should the worker share information with relatives who may be affected? Who has the primary claim to privacy and information in such situations? If the worker errs too much to one side or another, the rights of other participants may be harmed. Or, consider the ethical problems faced by social workers in adoption cases as the rights of adopted persons to information about their natural parents have been clarified. At one time, adoptive parents were assured that such knowledge would not be shared with the adoptee. But today, court decisions and legislative enactments in some states support the rights of adopted persons to such information. As a result, social workers are in a quandary. Do the rights of adoptive parents (to confidentiality) or those of the adoptees (to information) take precedence? And what about the rights of the natural parents?

Protection of Society's Interest

Sometimes it is difficult to balance society's interests with a client's interests. If a client tells a social worker that he committed a bank robbery, the social worker needs to weigh his obligations to the client against his obligations to society. Social control is a function of every social worker, but so is the maintenance of a helping relationship. If the worker cannot pursue both, to which function must he give priority? Would the same ethical considerations apply if the client were a part-time prostitute in a locality where prostitution is against the law? Can law-breaking be overlooked if clients are making progress toward the attainment of their own goals and they are not physically harming anyone else?

Another social worker had to face the dilemma posed by the following situation. A young man organized a youth gang that provided the neighborhood with many services, including security services for elderly people who formerly had been victims of attack and even murder. Thus, he helped control violence and assaults in the community. But, this young man also intimidated local storeowners and obtained small payoffs from them. The social worker was aware of both types of activities. Was it in the community's best interest to tolerate this young man's illegal activities which indirectly guaranteed peace and nonviolence in the neighborhood or was it preferable to turn him in to the police and thus permit the return of violence against older people?

The "Least Harm" Principle

Sometimes social workers are confronted by problems which permit only harmful options. Regardless of the choices made by either the social worker or the client, inevitably there will be harm to one person or another; perhaps even to the client or social worker. While common sense would suggest using the least harmful choice, this choice does not always avoid an ethical problem. Such a problem was faced by a social worker working with a family of five young children between the ages of three months and eight years whose parents were killed last week in an airplane accident. The children are now located temporarily in an emergency shelter since they have no relatives who can take care of them. Long term arrangements must be made for their care. The following options are under consideration: (1) a children's institution which could accommodate all five children or (2) foster homes pending adoptions. But no foster home is prepared to take more than two children. The social work staff is of the general opinion that an institutional placement is more harmful than a foster home, especially for the younger children. On the other hand, there is awareness that once the brothers and sisters are placed in separate foster homes they are unlikely to ever live together again as a family. The conflict facing the social worker here is between the "least harm" principle and the family maintenance principle.

While social workers will generally choose the least harm intervention, this choice is not inevitable and does not always lead to avoidance of the ethical dilemma. One may not always know what action will be the least harmful and some least harmful actions may not lead to ethically desirable action. Foster homes for the above family may be the least harmful choice at this time, but in a society which values the family this may not be the best choice from an ethical viewpoint.

SUMMARY

In this chapter we have examined the characteristics of decision-making through the use of a general decision-making model. With a focus on the worker and the ethical aspects of social work practice, our emphasis has been upon the selection of strategies and options which offer the best and most ethical alternative.

Four major sources from which social workers derive ethical decisions were examined including philosophical values, professional codes of ethics, practice wisdom and awareness and personal professional experience. In regard to philosophical values two basic ethical stances were identified: (1) teleological—the justification of ethical decisions on the basis of their consequences; and (2) deontological—the belief that actions are inherently right or wrong, apart from their consequences.

Professional codes of ethics as well as practice wisdom were explored in relation to their contributions to and limitations on ethical decision-making. Further, we reviewed the contributions of self-awareness and professional experience to the ethical decision-making of individual practitioners.

An examination and assessment of options and alternatives in ethical decision-making considered both efficiency and effectiveness criteria, the protection of clients' rights, and the protection of society's interests. Finally, we reviewed the fact that even the "least harm" principle does not always enable social workers to avoid ethical problems and dilemmas.

EXERCISES

1. Refugees are once again on the social agenda. There are various suggestions about limiting the number to be admitted and offering social services to those admitted. Examine the policy and program options from the point of view of the various ethical schools mentioned in the text.

2. The legislature of your state has been alarmed by the sharp rise in the number of children born to mentally retarded young adults. Even when these infants are not defective (and many are not), most of these retarded parents cannot give their infants the necessary care so that the children must be placed in foster homes at great expense to the public budget. A bill has been introduced by a group of powerful state senators, calling for mandatory sterilization of all mentally retarded men and women, twelve years of age

and older. They argue that this is an effective, efficient, and painless way of taking care of this problem. You have been asked by the local NASW chapter to prepare testimony in opposition to the bill. In your testimony you will be mindful that considerations of efficiency and effectiveness cannot be dismissed out of hand in these days of shrinking welfare budgets. Yet you might argue that ethical considerations are sometimes even more important. Remember, you are trying to convince legislators, not social workers.

3. Take one of the exemplars in Appendix A. Identify all the options available. Evaluate and assess them from an ethical point of view so that you can determine which is "best."

5 Guides to Ethical Decision-Making

Though social workers should never feel easy about ethical ·dilemmas and ethical problems, they must learn to cope with them. In prior chapters we have examined ethics in general, professional ethics in social work practice, professional dilemmas in postindustrial society, and principles of ethical decision-making. In this chapter we will present various ideas which have aided social workers in their quest for more effective ethical decision-making. These are neither magic formulae nor certain prescriptions, but they are guides which may point the way.

It is important to remember that ethical decision-making in social work takes place within the context of professional values. These support the "worth, dignity, and uniqueness of all persons as well as their rights and opportunities . . . (and) . . . foster conditions that promote these values" (NASW Code of Ethics, Preamble). Essentially, the social work value system reflects a democratic ethic which provides for individual and group fulfillment, respect for individuals and their differences, while recognizing the need for mutual aid and societal supports so that all persons can attain their maximum potential. Finding the proper balance between the opportunities and responsibilities of the individual and those of the community is a dilemma that is not unique to social workers. But within this balance, ethical decisions clearly follow a democratic ethos.

The subject of ethical decision-making is far too complex to permit developing a simple "how to" model. Nevertheless we want

79

to suggest a number of steps which we believe will contribute to strengthening the ethical decision-making ability of social workers. However, first a word of caution. Even those who reject a relativistic approach to ethics will agree that in practice there are no ethical rules which hold under all situations. For example, it is wrong to lie; but if we had lived in Nazi Germany and the Gestapo had come to our door looking for Jews, it would have been most ethical to deny that we were hiding Jews. This does not invalidate the value of truthfulness, but does suggest that there are probably exceptions for every ethic.

Our tentative paradigm for ethical decision-making includes the following steps:

1. **Clarification of one's own values.**
2. **Clarification of society's values.**
3. **Involvement of clients in decision-making.**
4. **Utilization of review mechanisms.**

Though this paradigm looks deceptively simple, there is need to explain and amplify it. We must also point to the limitations and pitfalls which beset social workers intent on strengthening their ethical decision-making. The focus in this paradigm, as throughout this book, is on the individual social worker. In a way this is unfortunate, even unfair, because it puts too great a burden on the individual professional. Though there is need for support systems to help the professional carry this burden, these are only now beginning to evolve. The revised NASW Code of Ethics is one professional mechanism which can help, but others need to be developed. The NASW adjudication procedure (see Appendix C) is another mechanism. But social workers urgently need additional support systems to help them in this area. Some of these will be suggested in the last section of this chapter.

STEP 1

Clarification of One's Own Values

"To thine own self be true, ... Thou canst not then be false to any man." This was Polonius' advice to Laertes in *Hamlet*. This same advice may also help social workers in their ethical decision-making. But to be true to oneself requires knowing what one really believes in. It is not enough to pay lip service to generalities and let it go at that. Instead the social worker must carefully scrutinize and clarify his or her values. For example, all reasonable men today value equality and abhor discrimination or exploitation on the basis of race, sex, or age. But how pervasive is this commitment to equality? Does it extend to persons with different sex preferences? With different lifestyles? Is it limited to humans or does it also extend to animals, as one British philosopher recently advocated (Singer 1979)? In a similar vein, those who argue in favor of abortion must clarify what they advocate. Until when should abortions be permitted? If it is held that abortions are permissible in the first two trimesters (through the sixth month), is it also permissible to kill a defective premature baby, born at the beginning of the sixth month? Does it make a difference whether this defective body is inside or outside of the womb? It is not our purpose here to take positions on these or other equally difficult moral questions. We merely raise these questions to point out the need for social workers to clarify their own value stances if they want to be true to themselves.

Clarifications of one's own values, though recommended as a first step in our paradigm, will not by itself solve value dilemmas. These dilemmas occur whenever the social worker holds two values which, in a given situation, give conflicting directives. For example, a social worker may hold the following values:

1. A woman has a right to decide whether or not she wants to carry pregnancy to full-term.
2. A social worker is obligated to practice within the policy established by the employing agency.[1]

In an earlier period, holding these two values placed many social workers before a serious ethical dilemma. And even today they may create an ethical dilemma for a worker who practices in an agency which does not permit its workers to assist clients in obtaining an abortion.

---

[1] As phrased, statement number 2 (see above) is a professional ethical statement and not a value. The corresponding value might be "obedience to one's employer."

Unless a worker can clarify his or her own value positions, ethical decision-making will lack substance, but will reflect whatever value positions happen to be in fashion at the time. There will be those who will argue that this, in itself, is not undesirable. However, our point is that value-fashions are not always reliable guides, especially in those unique situations where there is no established position.

STEP 2

Clarification of Society's Values

Radical changes in societal values have occurred within the lifetime of many social workers. Value positions which their parents or grandparents considered sacred have been swept away or altered so much that they are no longer recognizable. Though changes in values around lifestyles and sexual relations usually gain attention, the most fundamental change has occurred with respect to equality. Not too long ago it was self-understood that not all people were equal. An aged person did not enjoy the same rights as a working person; women were inferior to men, and whites were thought to be better than everybody else. Serious and respectable people propounded these views openly. Public policy was designed to reflect and support these values. It does not require any discussion here to point out the changes that have occurred. While racism, sexism, and ageism still exist in our society, these are no longer accorded respect and recognition.

Changes have occurred not only with respect to the equality-value but with respect to many other values. To the extent that ethical behavior is a reflection of what society values, the social worker must know where society stands. "Knowing" does not mean that the social worker should follow blindly. Following societal norms becomes especially problematic when a society accepts values which usually are disvalued. For example, must a social worker who practices in a totalitarian police state accept the currently popular values which include suppression of all political enemies—or does such a worker have an obligation to higher values? Here we must refer to our earlier discussion on the philosophical bases of professional ethics. We would maintain that societal values will not always give answers. There may be situations when a social worker is not only justified, but obligated to act in ways contrary to societal directives. But in every instance the worker has an obligation to clarify the current state of societal values.

STEP 3

Involvement of Clients in Decision-making

The first two elements dealt with clarification, understanding, and knowing. The next several elements will be concerned with things social workers do in their day-by-day practice, with elements which will contribute to more effective ethical decision-making.

Client's Role. Ethical problems will occur less frequently when clients are fully involved in decision-making. Of course, there will always be limitations on client involvement in decision-making due to age, incapacity, or involuntary settings, but the principle of maximum participation is not invalidated even when it is limited. However, maximum client participation in decision-making does not guarantee ethical decision-making. The client may "decide" in a way that is contrary to the professional ethics, as indicated in the following exemplar.

5.1: Ms. Epps wants a white worker

The Family Service intake worker had assigned Ms. Garland, a Black social worker, to work with Ms. Epps, a white client. During her initial session with Ms. Garland, Ms. Epps requested reassignment to another worker since she felt uncomfortable discussing her problems with a Black woman.

In this case, the client decided to ask for a social worker from her own ethnic group. Other clients might ask for a woman or a man, a lesbian or gay worker, an Italian or a Jewish worker. What are the ethical implications in agreeing or disagreeing with such a request?

Would it make an ethical difference if research showed that for certain problems a social worker from the same background is more effective than one from a different background?

Empowerment. Some clients need additional help before they can fully participate in decision-making. One useful technique is empowerment. Empowerment has been defined as the social work process which assists persons who belong to a stigmatized or damaged social category to develop their interpersonal skills so that they can more adequately fill valued social roles. The process involves giving power to the powerless so that they can gain greater control over their lives and their environment. A person who feels that he controls his or her destiny, who feels a sense of power over events, who recognizes and experiences an ability to influence the environment, such a person will also raise questions, ask for explanations, and participate in making decisions that affect the future. In short, such a person will serve as a check and balance to what might otherwise be the exclusive decision-making of the social worker.

Two exemplars follow. They illustrate the situation of members of stigmatized or damaged groups who cannot fully participate in the social work decision-making process without empowerment.

5.2:   The fears of a holocaust survivor

Mr. Lippman recently asked a social agency to help his wife. According to him, his wife has been having great difficulty functioning as a homemaker. In the intake interview, he explained that Mrs. Lippman was a survivor of the holocaust. Though she survived those terrible years in Nazi Europe, she lost her mother and father, brother and sisters, all of her cousins, uncles and aunts. Shortly after liberation she married him, a fellow concentration camp survivor. Together they migrated to the U.S. in the late 1940s.

Mrs. Lippman has always tried to keep a low profile in her family, as well as in the community, for fear that some tragedy might occur again to her and her family. For example, she does not vote in elections because she fears that her name on the voters' rolls might lead to her being executed some time in the future.

5.3: Black and unemployed

Gus Thompson is Black and twenty-two years old. He has
had many jobs since he graduated from high school, but has
been unable to stay on any job more than three months. It
seems that Blacks are always the first to get laid off. For more
than a year Gus has been walking the streets, looking for work.
He is convinced that there are no jobs for Blacks. He is angry
and disappointed. He feels bitter and sees no good in his future.
Lately he has stopped looking for work and just hangs out on
the block, together with many of his friends who are in the
same situation as he. At times he feels that there is no point to
continue living.

There are many differences between Mrs. Lippman and Mr.
Thompson. She is white, Jewish, and past middle age; he is Black,
Christian, and young. But both feel alienated and powerless, and
feel that they are out of control of their life. A social worker will
find it difficult to involve either in the social work process without employing empowerment. Only when Mrs. Lippman and Mr.
Thompson are in better control of themselves and their lives will
they be able to make many of the decisions which they now cannot
make.

Contracting.   The third element in client-involvement is contracting. By contract we refer to a "consensual, mutual agreement
and acceptance of reciprocal obligations and responsibilities, with
a promise to perform certain tasks and to deliver certain goods
within some time period" (Siporin 1975:208). The establishment of
a contract between a client and social worker limits and clarifies the
nature of the help sought and the kinds of tasks which will be undertaken by each in order to attain specified outcomes. Such a contract,
by identifying the specific areas of service, helps to limit the ethical
problems facing a social worker—limit but not eliminate. The
example of Ms. Turner's request for help illustrates this point.

5.4: Ms. Turner's daughter or husband?

Ms. Turner has come to the Suburban Family Service
because she has had problems with her twelve-year-old
daughter, Cecile. Cecile does not listen to her, sometimes

insults her father, stays out late with her friends, and does not take care of her clothing. Mr. LaMartine, her social worker, concluded after exploring these problems with her that (1) Cecile's problems are within the normal range for a girl of this age and (2) that there appeared to be indications of serious conflict between Mr. and Ms. Turner.

Before continuing, the worker has to negotiate a contract with Ms. Turner. He will want to share with her his findings, but the decision whether or not to work on her marital problems rests with Ms. Turner. On the other hand, if Ms. Turner insists that she only wants help with her problem with Cecile the worker needs to determine whether work on this problem is professionally justifiable. In other words, contracting does not release the worker from decision-making, but introduces a truly reciprocal relationship in which professional judgment plays an important part.

These three steps (client involvement, empowerment, and contract) will refocus the decision-making problem from one that is exclusively or primarily in the hands of the worker to one that includes a reciprocal relationship where both client and professional participate with equal force and equal responsibility. While such a refocus will not eliminate ethical problems, it should do much to limit their range and intensity.

STEP 4

Utilization of Review Mechanisms

Review mechanisms are no longer dreams or ideals. In this age of consumerism and accountability, review is a necessity for any profession that wishes to survive as a profession. But it has particular significance for the area of ethical decision-making. For a long time social workers have used informal peer review as a mechanism to check whether their impressions agreed with those of their colleagues. However, informal discussions around lunch are no substitute for formal disciplined reviews which focus on the professional performance of a colleague.

Accountability and Sensitization Techniques

In addition to the steps which an individual practitioner can undertake to ensure his own ethical decision-making, there are external devices which individual social workers can utilize to help themselves. All social agencies and the social workers employed by them are accountable, that is, they are responsible for their actions. Accountability systems are necessary to implement this accountability in responsible ways. According to Hoshino (1978:299) these systems have the following features:

1. A sensing or monitoring mechanism.
2. Sampling.
3. Indicators from which inferences about quality can be made.
4. Criteria or standards in regard to quality.
5. A feedback system to provide information about the performance of the larger system.

Accountability systems generally focus on practice performance, but they can also be utilized to monitor ethical decision-making performance.

Peer Review and Consultation

Peer review can be a helpful device to enable social work practitioners to test their ethical decision-making against the perspectives of their professional peers. In the past, social workers have utilized both formal and informal groups to review their professional practice decisions. Such groups can also be formed to focus specifically upon ethical decision-making. Or on-going peer review groups which focus upon the quality of performance may also pay attention to ethical decision-making.

Consultants can be used to educate staff members to the intricacies of ethical questions and decision-making, as a sensitizer to ethical problems and as an aid toward better ethical decision-making.

Private practice raises special considerations in regard to ethical decision-making. Private practice places a social worker in an isolated situation in which the opportunity for interchange with fellow professionals may be limited. It is also a situation in which the controls and accountability of the social worker depend solely upon the sensitivity and knowledge of the individual practitioner. While there are peer pressures upon social workers employed in agencies, these are much less in evidence for the social worker in private practice. Private practitioners may want to organize among themselves peer review and consultation services specifically geared to ethical decision-making in order to ensure that their professional decisions will be of the highest ethical level.

Ombudsmen, Administrative Review and Appeals Procedures

Additional techniques which may be helpful in assisting social workers in making ethical decisions include the establishment of ombudsmen, and realistic administrative review and appeals procedures which make it possible for clients to express their views about potential or actual actions of their workers. These general accountability devices will also serve to sensitize social workers to potential ethical problems and, in some cases, may serve to rectify ethical errors which social workers have made.

Committee on the Ethics of Social Work Practice

Another mechanism is a Committee on the Ethics of Social Work Practice, analogous to the Committee on the Rights of Human Subjects, which exists in every research organization. This committee would be a regular staff committee in a social agency, staffed by a representative group of professional social workers. Practitioners who are aware of ethical problems may bring them to this committee for consultation. This committee could serve as a formal means for helping social workers to think through thorny ethical questions which occur to them in their everyday practice.

National Association of Social Workers

The National Association of Social Workers can also encourage the further development of ethical decision-making within the profession. The professional association can do the following:

1. Form formal groups for the study and review of ethical decisions arising out of actual social work practice experiences.
2. Focus on these issues at conferences and in continuing education programs.
3. Develop a data bank.

In regard to the third suggestion above, it is desirable that social workers begin to collect data on ethical decision-making, including errors and embarrassments. The collection of this data will be helpful to practitioners and students. This information will set forth the ethical quandaries experienced by social workers, along with the preferred solutions, and the results achieved. These data will be helpful in the creation of case materials so necessary for the systematic development of sorely needed social work knowledge.[2]

SUMMARY

In this final chapter we have presented ideas and techniques which have aided social workers in their search for more effective ethical decision-making. The values of the social work profession form the background for the ethical decision-making of individual practitioners.

We presented a tentative paradigm for ethical decision-making. This process begins with clarification of one's own values. Knowledge of what one really believes is an inescapable basic step for social workers seeking to improve their ethical decision-making. Beyond the clarification of one's own personal value stances, it is of importance that social workers clarify for themselves the values of our society and of the various subgroups with which they work. Clarification of societal and group values can help social workers to be more aware as to potential value conflicts in regard to their own values and also in regard to the clash of societal and client values.

---

[2] We are indebted to Dean Joseph L. Vigilante of Adelphi University School of Social Work for this idea and for pointing out the need for creation of a precedents literature in the area of ethical decision-making analogous to the development of case law.

We have suggested that the full involvement of clients—recognizing the possible limitations of age, incapacity, or involuntary settings—can be helpful in enhancing the ethical decision-making of social workers. But this too is not foolproof and as we saw in this this chapter, clients like Ms. Epps may make decisions which are contrary to professional ethics. Empowerment and contracting can serve also as aids as they delimit and clarify the nature of the social worker-client relationship and the tasks to be undertaken.

Other mechanisms can also be useful for the enhancement of ethical decision-making by social workers. The utilization of review mechanisms, accountability and sensitization techniques, peer review and consultation, can serve to enhance ethical social work practice. Several types of review and consultation can be employed including the use of consultants, ombudsmen, administrative review and appeals procedures, and committees on the ethics of social work practice. The development of formal study groups and the emphases of conferences and continuing education can also contribute. The creation of a data bank on ethical decision-making and the creation of a case literature can build systematic knowledge and understanding by utilizing the everyday experiences of social workers to build an ever more precise understanding of ethical decision-making by social workers and to foster an ever more ethical social work profession and professionals.

EXERCISES

1. Identify two ethical dilemma situations from your own personal or professional experience. How could the guides suggested in Chapter 5 have helped you make better ethical decisions?

2. List several professional actions by social workers which you believe to be clearly outstanding examples of ethical behaviors. On what bases did you make your evaluations?

3. How can social workers help each other even more than they now do to make high quality ethical decisions?

4. Draft a revision of two points of the present NASW Code of Ethics. Debate the pros and cons of your suggested revision with a colleague or fellow student.

Further Readings*

Bermant, Gordon; Kelman, Herbert C.; and Warwick, Donald P., eds. *The Ethics of Social Intervention.* New York: Wiley and Sons, 1978.

A number of experts consider various ethical aspects of social intervention. Stolz's chapter on ethical issues in behavior modification is especially important for social workers.

Callahan, Daniel. "Contemporary Biomedical Ethics." *New England Journal of Medicine* 302 (1980): 1228–33.

Previews some of the issues which biomedical ethics must face during this decade. Examines the implications of the excessive focus on individual rights, both in ethics and jurisprudence. Questions the idea of a single-ethic morality for a balanced and useful professional ethic.

Howe, Elizabeth. "Public Professions and the Private Model of Professionalism." *Social Work* 25 (1980): 179–91.

Examines the codes of ethics of a number of professions, including the NASW Codes of 1967 and 1979. Finds a pronounced shift toward the private focus in the most recent social work code. Only medicine, among the professional codes surveyed, has greater emphasis on the individual and less on the common good.

* See Bibliography for Complete Reference Listing.

Keith-Lucas, Alan. "Ethics in Social Work." *Encyclopedia of Social Work*. Washington: NASW, 1977, pp. 350–5.

A concise summary article that discusses the place of ethics in social work practice.

Levy, Charles. *Social Work Ethics*. New York: Human Sciences Press, 1976.

A basic consideration of the history of social work ethics, prepared by the social work educator who later chaired the NASW committee which drafted the 1979 NASW Code of Ethics.

Lickona, Thomas, ed. *Moral Development and Behavior: Theory, Research, and Social Issues*. New York: Holt, Rinehart and Winston, 1976.

A collection of articles on theoretical perspectives and research on moral development and behavior with an exploration of morality and social issues, including articles on moral understanding and clinical practice, public policy debate, social ecology of violence. A demanding and difficult text.

Loewenberg, Frank M. "Professional Values and Professional Ethics in Social Work Education." In *Educating the Baccalaureate Social Worker*, eds. Betty L. Baer and Ron Federico. Cambridge: Ballinger, 1978, pp. 115–29.

A fuller discussion of the relation between professional values and professional ethics by one of the authors of this book.

McCann, Charles W., and Cutler, Jane Park. "Ethics and the Alleged Unethical." *Social Work* 24 (1979): 5–8.

Between 1955 and 1977 a total of 154 complaints involving alleged unethical conduct by social workers was processed by the appropriate organs of NASW. This article analyzes the issues and trends involved and makes recommendations about changes necessary in the NASW Code of Ethics.

Pilseker, Carleton. "Values: A Problem for Everyone." *Social Work* 23 (1978): 54–7.

Argues that social workers cannot be non-judgmental and that they should not attempt to be so.

Reamer, Frederic G. "Fundamental Ethical Issues in Social Work."
Social Service Review 53 (1979): 229–43.

A first attempt to consider the implications of Gewirth's
Reason and Morality for social workers. Raises questions about
the way ethical criteria are established and applied in social
work practice.

Salzberger, Ronald Paul. "Casework and a Client's Right to Self-
Determination." *Social Work* 24 (1979): 398–400.

Examines the concept of self-determination and argues that
clients who are incapacitated in some manner do not lose their
right to self-determination.

Sammons, Catherine C. "Ethical Issues in Genetic Intervention."
Social Work 23 (1978): 237–42.

Genetic interventions and diagnostic tests present the social
worker with ethical dilemmas because they may conflict with
social work values.

Smith, William H. "Ethical, Social and Professional Issues in
Patient's Access to Psychological Test Reports." *Bulletin of the
Menninger Clinic* 42, 2 (1978): 150–5.

Even though the author recognizes that the trend is toward
opening up records to patients, he develops the arguments
against this practice.

Tancredi, Laurence R., and Slaby, Andrew E. *Ethical Policy in
Mental Health Care.* New York: Prodist, 1977.

Focuses on the way power is distributed and used to fulfill the
goal of improving the population's health, with special emphasis on ethical problems facing mental health workers.

Vigilante, Joseph. "Between Values and Science: Education for the
Profession During a Moral Crisis or Is Proof Truth?" *Journal
of Education for Social Work* 10 (Fall 1974): 107–15.

A value conflict has emerged between humanitarianism and
individualism. Current interpretations of individualism challenge the social work value of mutuality.

Wilson, Suanna J. *Confidentiality in Social Work*. New York: Free Press, 1978.

A comprehensive, book-length analysis of all aspects of confidentiality in social work practice. Implications of the Federal Privacy Act and various relevant court decisions for social work practice are examined.

For additional current material of interest, consult the following journals:

Bulletin of the Menninger Clinic
Ethics
Hastings Center Report
Philosophy and Public Affairs

Bibliography

Bartlett, Harriet M. *The Common Base of Social Work Practice.* New York: NASW, 1970.

Bermant, Gordon; Kelman, Herbert C.; Warwick, Donald P., eds. *The Ethics of Social Intervention.* New York: Wiley and Sons, 1978.

Bernstein, Saul. "Self-Determination: King or Citizen in the Realm of Values." *Social Work* 5, 1 (1960): 3–8.

Bok, J. Sissela. *Lying: Moral Choice in Public and Private Life.* New York: Pantheon Books, 1978.

Callahan, Daniel. "Contemporary Biomedical Ethics." *New England Journal of Medicine* 302 (1980: 1228–33.

Diener, Edward, and Crandall, Rick. *Ethics in Social and Behavioral Research.* Chicago: University of Chicago Press, 1978.

Fitzgerald, F. Scott. *The Crack-Up.* New York: New Directions Paperback, 1936.

Frankena, William K. *Ethics.* 2nd ed. Englewood Cliffs: Prentice-Hall, 1973.

Gewirth, Alan. *Reason and Morality.* Chicago: University of Chicago Press, 1978.

Greenwood, Ernest. "Attributes of a Profession." *Social Work* 2, 3 (July 1957): 45–55.

Halleck, S. L. *The Politics of Therapy.* New York: Science House, 1971.

Halmos, P. *Faith of the Counselors.* London: Constable, 1965.

Hazard, Geoffrey Jr. *Ethics in the Practice of Law.* New Haven: Yale University Press, 1978.

Hoshino, George. "Social Services: The Problem of Accountability." In *Social Administration*, ed. Simon Slavin. New York: Haworth Press, 1978, pp. 299–309.

Howe, Elizabeth. "Public Professions and the Private Model of Professionalism." *Social Work* 25 (1980): 179–91.

Keith-Lucas, Alan. "Ethics in Social Work." *Encyclopedia of Social Work*. Washington: NASW, 1977, pp. 350–5.

Levenstein, Phyllis. "Ethical Considerations in Home-Based Programs." Paper presented at National Symposium on Home-Based Care for Children and Families. Iowa City, Iowa: ERIC Document ED 181997, 1979. Mimeographed.

Levy, Charles. *Social Work Ethics*. New York: Human Sciences Press, 1976.

Lickona, Thomas, ed. *Moral Development and Behavior: Theory, Research, and Social Issues*. New York: Holt, Rinehart and Winston, 1976.

Loewenberg, Frank M. *Fundamentals of Social Intervention*. New York: Columbia University Press, 1977.

————. "Professional Values and Professional Ethics in Social Work Education." In *Educating the Baccalaureate Social Worker*, eds. Betty L. Baer and Ron Federico. Cambridge: Ballinger, 1978, pp. 115–29.

————. *Burnout and Turnover: Are They the Same?* Forthcoming.

Loewenberg, Frank M., and Dolgoff, Ralph, eds. *The Practice of Social Intervention*. Itasca, Ill.: F. E. Peacock Publishers, 1972.

Maslow, Abraham. *The Farther Reaches of Human Nature*. New York: Penguin Books, 1962.

McCann, Charles W., and Cutler, Jane Park. "Ethics and the Alleged Unethical." *Social Work* 24 (1979): 5–8.

Nader, Ralph; Petkas, Peter J.; and Blackwell, Kate. *Whistle Blowing*. New York: Grossman Publishers, 1972.

Nietzsche, Friedrich. *Beyond Good and Evil*. Translated by Helen Zimmern. London: George Allen and Unwin, 1923.

Perlman, Helen H. "Self-Determination: Reality or Illusion?" *Social Service Review* 39 (1965): 410–22.

————. "Believing and Doing: Values in Social Work Education." *Social Casework* 57 (1976): 381–90.

Pilseker, Carlton. "Values: A Problem for Everyone." *Social Work* 23 (1978): 54–7.

Pumphrey, Muriel. *The Teaching of Values and Ethics in Social Work Education.* New York: CSWE, 1959.

Rawls, John. *A Theory of Justice.* Cambridge: Harvard University Press, 1971.

Reamer, Frederic G. "Fundamental Ethical Issues in Social Work." *Social Service Review* 53 (1979): 229–43.

Salzberger, Ronald Paul. "Casework and a Client's Right to Self-Determination." *Social Work* 24 (1979): 398–400.

Sammons, Catherine C. "Ethical Issues in Genetic Intervention." *Social Work* 23 (1978): 237–42.

Schultz, Leroy G. "Ethical Issues in Treating Sexual Dysfunction." *Social Work* 20 (March 1975): 126–8.

Simon, Sidney B.; Howe, Leland W.; and Kirschenbaum, Howard. *Values Clarification: A Handbook of Practical Strategies for Teachers and Students.* New York: Hart Publishing Co., 1978.

Singer, Peter. *Practical Ethics.* Cambridge: Cambridge University Press, 1979.

Siporin, Max. *Introduction to Social Work Practice.* New York: Macmillan Publishing Co., 1975.

Smith, William H. "Ethical, Social, and Professional Issues in Patient's Access to Psychological Test Reports." *Bulletin of the Menninger Clinic* 42, 2 (1978): 150–5.

Tancredi, Laurence R., and Slaby, Andrew E. *Ethical Policy in Mental Health Care.* New York: Prodist, 1977.

Towle, Charlotte. *Common Human Needs.* New York: NASW, 1965.

Vigilante, Joseph. "Between Values and Science: Education for the Profession During a Moral Crisis or Is Proof Truth?" *Journal of Education for Social Work* 10 (Fall 1974): 107–15.

Williams, Robin M. Jr. "Individual and Group Values." *The Annals* 371 (1967): 20–37.

Wilson, Suanna J. *Confidentiality in Social Work.* New York: Free Press, 1978.

Wispe, Lauren. *Altruism, Sympathy, and Helping.* New York: Academic Press, 1978.

Yelaja, Shankar A. "Teaching Values and Ethics in Social Work Through a Debate Format." Paper presented at the Annual Program Meeting of the Council on Social Work Education. Los Angeles, March 1980. Mimeographed.

Appendix A

ADDITIONAL EXEMPLARS OF ETHICAL DILEMMAS

In gathering material for this book, we came across many more illustrations than we could use in the text. Some of these appear below and may be used as additional exercises.

AA. Carla Fernandez has a long history of heroin addiction and prostitution. She has just given birth for the first time. The hospital medical staff is concerned about Carla's ability to care properly for the baby, in view of her history and her present lack of interest in the infant.

What are Carla's rights? The baby's? What responsibility does the social worker have in this situation? Would it make a difference if the senior staff member had been a Chicano, like Carla?

BB. George White is wanted by the FBI for suspected kidnapping, rape, and murder. The FBI poster describes him and indicates that he may present himself at a mental health clinic for treatment. You are on intake duty and a man with all the identifying characteristics of George White comes in, requesting treatment. What should you do?

CC. The Heymans already have two daughters. Mrs. Heyman is again pregnant. They have just been told by their social worker that the amniocentesis test showed a negative Tay-Sachs and that they would have another girl. Neither parent wants another girl. They request your help to arrange for an immediate abortion.

Is it ethical to abort a female foetus just because the parents have their mind set on a boy?

DD. Estes Hodges is a supervisor in a Department of Social Services in a western county. He is slotted for promotion to a managerial position in a branch office which will mean much more responsibility and income for him and his family. Concurrently, a friend who is a colleague has been taking a stand publicly complaining about the services provided by the agency. As a result, many employees of the agency ostracize him and it is well-known that the agency director is very angry and looking for an opportunity to fire him. Mr. Hodges' colleague approaches him privately to get advice and help so that he will not lose his job. If Mr. Hodges befriends him, it is certain the director will find out about it and he will not get the promotion.

What conflicting values are at stake here? What options for action are available, public and private? What are the potential costs? For whom? What would you do?

EE. A school evaluation and referral unit staffed by a psychiatrist, psychologist, and social worker is directed by an educator. The human service professionals are viewed as ancillary workers in the system and teachers are the final decision-makers. Other agencies provide on the basis of signed consent forms social histories. There is seldom supervision of the content included in these histories and, although the focus is the schoolchild, there are statements about the psychiatric hospitalization of parents, alcoholism, arrests, and other information. Although the social and psychological reports are termed confidential, the fact is that everyone in the system— Board members and staff, including paraprofessionals who know the parents in the neighborhood—has free access to the school and the files.

Do different professional disciplines have differing professional perspectives on confidentiality? Under what circumstances should lay persons, other professionals, paraprofessionals have access to confidential files?

FF.   Sal DiBenedetto has been referred to your agency because of a serious disability and he needs placement in a residential facility with rehabilitation services. He formerly was in difficulty with several agencies and another facility where he was viewed as hostile and uncooperative. You have placed persons in the facility which is needed by Mr. DiBenedetto and have performed certain services for their staff. However, you know you will use up all your points if you send them a patient who cannot be "handled." There is no other facility with the needed services and you have other clients who also need to be sent to this particular institution.

How do you balance responsibility to Mr. DiBenedetto against the needs of your other clients, present and future?

GG.   An assessment center for the learning disabled was placed so as to provide accessibility for the poor. Because of the location of the Center, middle-class parents refuse to go there. Referrals, therefore, from this public agency are being made to a private practitioner group more accessible for the middle-class parents and their children. This fact is being interpreted by some middle-class persons as proof that the public system cannot work and thus the public system should increase its utilization of private consultants and referrals to private practitioners.

What are the ethical dilemmas in this situation? Can you place the dilemmas in order of priority? What would you do?

In the following exemplars: What is the dilemma? What is your assessment of the situation? What would you suggest be done? How would you evaluate whether or not you did the right thing?

HH.   You are a field instructor for a School of Social Work. You have a client who has applied to the school and without asking you has given your name as a reference. You think the client is not really capable at this time of taking advantage of the learning opportunity. In discussion, it becomes clear your client views your actions as either an act of love or an act of rejection and feels that attendance at school will allow him the first real opportunity for mature action as an adult, is an important career decision, and so forth.

II.   Henry is an illegal alien who lives with a group of three other illegal aliens in an apartment. They all work very long hours in a sweatshop. To obtain more money in order to pay off a blackmailer, he has been burglarizing apartments in the area. Recently, Henry suffered an anxiety attack at work and was taken by friends to a private social agency for treatment because they were afraid of going to any public agency where they probably would be reported to the Immigration and Naturalization authorities. You are the social worker in the private social agency. If you report the burglaries, you will endanger Henry, his family's chances of coming to the United States to join him, the group of illegal immigrants with whom he lives and those friends of his in the community who have been helping him survive.

JJ.   You are a social worker in a hospital setting and learn that confidential information about patients is being sent routinely via computer to insurance companies despite the hospital's formal statements protecting confidentiality. Physicians, psychologists, nurses, and other social workers on the team on which you serve have all come to accept this as a fact of life and tell you to forget it when you raise the problem with them individually.

KK.   A young pregnant woman comes to a medical clinic requesting amniocentesis because she is fearful she is the carrier of Tay-Sachs disease. The amniocentesis is performed and several weeks later it is discovered she has a good chance of delivering a child with a congenital defect. When she hears the test results she tells the social worker she will keep the information to herself and asks the worker not to tell her husband the results because she is the patient and came herself for assistance. She wants to keep the information secret because there is also a chance the foetus will be healthy.

LL.   You are a school social worker in an affluent community and discover that there is a group of teenagers involved in extortion of younger kids. When you report this to your supervisor, you discover that several of the teenagers are the children of extremely prominent, wealthy, and influential members of the community including a former School Board chairman who is involved in business dealings with the School principal.

MM.   The mayor of your town has a tough budget stance which has meant fewer garbage pickups all over town. You are a social worker in a settlement house in a poor neighborhood. A committee you serve decides to dump garbage on the lawn of the mayor's home despite your questioning the wisdom of this action.

NN.   A social worker in an agency has been working with a group of young adults for some time. A new member is to be introduced into the group and he is known to the social worker to be a "womanizer" and in the past has had several sadistic relationships. On the one hand, the group is good for the young man; on the other, there is potential danger.

Appendix B

CODES OF ETHICS

1. National Association of Social Workers

Preamble

This code is intended to serve as a guide to the everyday conduct of members of the social work profession and as a basis for the adjudication of issues in ethics when the conduct of social workers is alleged to deviate from the standards expressed or implied in this code. It represents standards of ethical behavior for social workers in professional relationships with those served, with colleagues, with employers, with other individuals and professions, and with the community and society as a whole. It also embodies standards of ethical behavior governing individual conduct to the extent that such conduct is associated with an individual's status and identity as a social worker.

This code is based on the fundamental values of the social work profession that include the worth, dignity, and uniqueness of all persons as well as their rights and opportunities. It is also based on the nature of social work, which fosters

This Code of Ethics as adopted by the 1979 NASW Delegate Assembly, effective July 1, 1980, is included here with the permission of the National Association of Social Workers.

conditions that promote these values.

In subscribing to and abiding by this code, the social worker is expected to view ethical responsibility in as inclusive a context as each situation demands and within which ethical judgement is required. The social worker is expected to take into consideration all the principles in this code that have a bearing upon any situation in which ethical judgement is to be exercised and professional intervention or conduct is planned. The course of action that the social worker chooses is expected to be consistent with the spirit as well as the letter of this code.

In itself, this code does not represent a set of rules that will prescribe all the behaviors of social workers in all the complexities of professional life. Rather, it offers general principles to guide conduct, and the judicious appraisal of conduct, in situations that have ethical implications. It provides the basis for making judgements about ethical actions before and after they occur. Frequently, the particular situation determines the ethical principles that apply and the manner of their application. In such cases, not only the particular ethical principles are taken into immediate consideration, but also the entire code and its

spirit. Specific applications of ethical principles must be judged within the context in which they are being considered. Ethical behavior in a given situation must satisfy not only the judgement of the individual social worker, but also the judgement of an unbiased jury of professional peers.

This code should not be used as an instrument to deprive any social worker of the opportunity or freedom to practice with complete professional integrity; nor should any disciplinary action be taken on the basis of this code without maximum provision for safeguarding the rights of the social worker affected.

The ethical behavior of social workers results not from edict, but from a personal commitment of the individual. This code is offered to affirm the will and zeal of all social workers to be ethical and to act ethically in all that they do as social workers.

The following codified ethical principles should guide social workers in the various roles and relationships and at the various levels of responsibility in which they function professionally. These principles also serve as a basis for the adjudication by the National Association of Social Workers of issues in ethics.

In subscribing to this code, social workers are required to cooperate in its implementation and abide by any disciplinary rulings based on it. They should also take adequate measures to discourage, prevent, expose, and correct the unethical conduct of colleagues. Finally, social workers should be equally ready to defend and assist colleagues unjustly charged with unethical conduct.

I. The Social Worker's Conduct and Comportment as a Social Worker

A. Propriety—The social worker should maintain high standards of personal conduct in the capacity or identity as social worker.

1. The private conduct of the social worker is a personal matter to the same degree as is any other person's, except when such conduct compromises the fulfillment of professional responsibilities.

2. The social worker should not participate in, condone, or be associated with dishonesty, fraud, deceit, or misrepresentation.

3. The social worker should distinguish clearly between statements and actions made as a private individual and as a representative of the social work profession or an organization or group.

B. Competence and Professional Development—The social worker should strive to become and remain proficient in professional practice and the performance of professional functions.

1. The social worker should accept responsibility or employment only on the basis of existing competence or the intention to acquire the necessary competence.

2. The social worker should not misrepresent professional qualifications, education, experience, or affiliations.

C. Service—The social worker should regard as primary the service obligation of the social work profession.

1. The social worker should retain ultimate responsibility for the quality and extent of the service that individual assumes, assigns, or performs.

2. The social worker should act to prevent practices that are inhumane or discriminatory against any person or group of persons.

D. Integrity—The social worker should act

in accordance with the highest standards of professional integrity and impartiality.

1. The social worker should be alert to and resist the influences and pressures that interfere with the exercise of professional discretion and impartial judgement required for the performance of professional functions.

2. The social worker should not exploit professional relationships for personal gain.

E. Scholarship and Research—The social worker engaged in study and research should be guided by the conventions of scholarly inquiry.

1. The social worker engaged in research should consider carefully its possible consequences for human beings.

2. The social worker engaged in research should ascertain that the consent of participants in the research is voluntary and informed, without any implied deprivation or penalty for refusal to participate, and with due regard for participants' privacy and dignity.

3. The social worker engaged in research should protect participants from unwarranted physical or mental discomfort, distress, harm, danger, or deprivation.

4. The social worker who engages in the evaluation of services or cases should discuss them only for professional purposes and only with persons directly and professionally concerned with them.

5. Information obtained about participants in research should be treated as confidential.

6. The social worker should take credit only for work actually done in connection with scholarly and research endeavors and credit contributions made by others.

II. The Social Worker's Ethical Responsibility to Clients

F. Primacy of Clients' Interests—The social worker's primary responsibility is to clients.

1. The social worker should serve clients with devotion, loyalty, determination, and the maximum application of professional skill and competence.

2. The social worker should not exploit relationships with clients for personal advantage, or solicit the clients of one's agency for private practice.

3. The social worker should not practice, condone, facilitate or collaborate with any form of discrimination on the basis of race, color, sex, sexual orientation, age, religion, national origin, marital status, political belief, mental or physical handicap, or any other preference or personal characteristic, condition or status.

4. The social worker should avoid relationships or commitments that conflict with the interests of clients.

5. The social worker should under no circumstances engage in sexual activities with clients.

6. The social worker should provide clients with accurate and complete information regarding the extent and nature of the services available to them.

7. The social worker should apprise clients of their risks, rights, opportunities, and obligations associated with social service to them.

8. The social worker should seek advice and counsel of colleagues and supervisors whenever such consultation is in the best interest of clients.

9. The social worker should terminate service to clients, and professional relationships with them, when such service and relationships are no longer required or no longer serve the clients' needs or interests.

10. The social worker should withdraw services precipitously only under unusual circumstances, giving careful consideration to all factors in the situation and taking care to minimize possible adverse effects.

11. The social worker who anticipates the termination or interruption of service to clients should notify clients promptly and seek the transfer, referral, or continuation of service in relation to the clients' needs and preferences.

G. Rights and Prerogatives of Clients—The social worker should make every effort to foster maximum self-determination on the part of clients.

1. When the social worker must act on behalf of a client who has been adjudged legally incompetent, the social worker should safeguard the interests and rights of that client.

2. When another individual has been legally authorized to act in behalf of a client, the social worker should deal with that person always with the client's best interest in mind.

3. The social worker should not engage in any action that violates or diminishes the civil or legal

reasonable, considerate and commensurate with the service performed and with due regard for the clients' ability to pay.

1. The social worker should not divide a fee or accept or give anything of value for receiving or making a referral.

III. The Social Worker's Ethical Responsibility to Colleagues

J. Respect, Fairness, and Courtesy—The social worker should treat colleagues with respect, courtesy, fairness, and good faith.

1. The social worker should cooperate with colleagues to promote professional interests and concerns.

2. The social worker should respect confidences shared by colleagues in the course of their professional relationships and transactions.

3. The social worker should create and maintain conditions of practice that facilitate ethical and competent professional performance by colleagues.

4. The social worker should treat with respect, and represent accurately and fairly, the qualifications, views, and findings of colleagues and use

rights of clients.

H. Confidentiality and Privacy—The social worker should respect the privacy of clients and hold in confidence all information obtained in the course of professional service.

1. The social worker should share with others confidences revealed by clients, without their consent, only for compelling professional reasons.

2. The social worker should inform clients fully about the limits of confidentiality in a given situation, the purposes for which information is obtained, and how it may be used.

3. The social worker should afford clients reasonable access to any official social work records concerning them.

4. When providing clients with access to records, the social worker should take due care to protect the confidences of others contained in those records.

5. The social worker should obtain informed consent of clients before taping, recording, or permitting third party observation of their activities.

I. Fees—When setting fees, the social worker should ensure that they are fair,

manner, on the basis of clearly enunciated criteria.

11. The social worker who has the responsibility for evaluating the performance of employees, supervisees, or students should share evaluations with them.

K. Dealing with Colleagues' Clients—The social worker has the responsibility to relate to the clients of colleagues with full professional consideration.

1. The social worker should not solicit the clients of colleagues.

2. The social worker should not assume professional responsibility for the clients of another agency or a colleague without appropriate communication with that agency or colleague.

3. The social worker who serves the clients of colleagues, during a temporary absence or emergency, should serve those clients with the same consideration as that afforded any client.

IV. The Social Worker's Ethical Responsibility to Employers and Employing Organizations.

L. Commitment to Employing Organiza-

appropriate channels to express judgements on these matters.

5. The social worker who replaces or is replaced by a colleague in professional practice should act with consideration for the interest, character, and reputation of that colleague.

6. The social worker should not exploit a dispute between a colleague and employers to obtain a position or otherwise advance the social worker's interest.

7. The social worker should seek arbitration or mediation when conflicts with colleagues require resolution for compelling professional reasons.

8. The social worker should extend to colleagues of other professions the same respect and cooperation that is extended to social work colleagues.

9. The social worker who serves as an employer, supervisor, or mentor to colleagues should make orderly and explicit arrangements regarding the conditions of their continuing professional relationship.

10. The social worker who has the responsibility for employing and evaluating the performance of other staff members, should fulfill such responsibility in a fair, considerate, and equitable

tion—The social worker should adhere to commitments made to the employing organization.

1. The social worker should work to improve the employing agency's policies and procedures, and the efficiency and effectiveness of its services.

2. The social worker should not accept employment or arrange student field placements in an organization which is currently under public sanction by NASW for violating personnel standards or imposing limitations on or penalties for professional actions on behalf of clients.

3. The social worker should act to prevent and eliminate discrimination in the employing organization's work assignments and in its employment policies and practices.

4. The social worker should use with scrupulous regard, and only for the purpose for which they are intended, the resources of the employing organization.

M. Maintaining the Integrity of the Profession—The social worker should uphold and advance the values, ethics, knowledge, and mission of the profession.

1. The social worker should protect and enhance the dignity and integrity of the profession and should be responsible and vigorous in discussion and criticism of the profession.

2. The social worker should take action through appropriate channels against unethical conduct by any other member of the profession.

3. The social worker should act to prevent the unauthorized and unqualified practice of social work.

4. The social worker should make no misrepresentation in advertising as to qualifications, competence, service, or results to be achieved.

N. Community Service—The social worker should assist the profession in making social services available to the general public.

1. The social worker should contribute time and professional expertise to activities that promote respect for the utility, the integrity, and the competence of the social work profession.

V. The Social Worker's Ethical Responsibility to the Social Work Profession

2. The social worker should support the formulation, development, enactment and implementation of social policies of concern to the profession.

O. Development of Knowledge—The social worker should take responsibility for identifying, developing, and fully utilizing knowledge for professional practice.

1. The social worker should base practice upon recognized knowledge relevant to social work.

2. The social worker should critically examine, and keep current with, emerging knowledge relevant to social work.

3. The social worker should contribute to the knowledge base of social work and share research knowledge and practice wisdom with colleagues.

VI. The Social Worker's Ethical Responsibility to Society

P. Promoting the General Welfare—The social worker should promote the general welfare of society.

1. The social worker should act to prevent and eliminate discrimination against any person or group on the basis of race, color, sex, sexual orientation, age, religion, national origin, marital status, political belief, mental or physical handicap, or any other preference or personal characteristic, condition, or status.

2. The social worker should act to ensure that all persons have access to the resources, services, and opportunities which they require.

3. The social worker should act to expand choice and opportunity for all persons, with special regard for disadvantaged or oppressed groups and persons.

4. The social worker should promote conditions that encourage respect for the diversity of cultures which constitute American society.

5. The social worker should provide appropriate professional services in public emergencies.

6. The social worker should advocate changes in policy and legislation to improve social conditions and to promote social justice.

7. The social worker should encourage informed participation by the public in shaping social policies and institutions.

Summary of Major Principles

I. THE SOCIAL WORKER'S CONDUCT AND COMPORTMENT AS A SOCIAL WORKER

   A. *Propriety*. The social worker should maintain high standards of personal conduct in the capacity or identity as social worker.

   B. *Competence and Professional Development*. The social worker should strive to become and remain proficient in professional practice and the performance of professional functions.

   C. *Service*. The social worker should regard as primary the service obligation of the social work profession.

   D. *Integrity*. The social worker should act in accordance with the highest standards of professional integrity.

   E. *Scholarship and Research*. The social worker engaged in study and research should be guided by the conventions of scholarly inquiry.

II. THE SOCIAL WORKER'S ETHICAL RESPONSIBILITY TO CLIENTS

   F. *Primacy of Clients' Interests*. The social worker's primary responsibility is to clients.

   G. *Rights and Prerogatives of Clients*. The social worker should make every effort to foster maximum self-determination on the part of clients.

   H. *Confidentiality and Privacy*. The social worker should respect the privacy of clients and hold in confidence all information obtained in the course of professional service.

   I. *Fees*. When setting fees, the social worker should ensure that they are fair, reasonable, considerate, and commensurate with the service performed and with due regard for the clients' ability to pay.

III. THE SOCIAL WORKER'S ETHICAL RESPONSIBILITY TO COLLEAGUES

   J. *Respect, Fairness, and Courtesy*. The social worker should treat colleagues with respect, courtesy, fairness, and good faith.

   K. *Dealing with Colleagues' Clients*. The social worker has the responsibility to relate to the clients of colleagues with full professional consideration.

IV. THE SOCIAL WORKER'S ETHICAL RESPONSIBILITY TO EMPLOYERS AND EMPLOYING ORGANIZA-TIONS

L. *Commitments to Employing Organizations.* The social worker should adhere to commitments made to the employing organizations.

V. THE SOCIAL WORKER'S ETHICAL RESPONSIBILITY TO THE SOCIAL WORK PROFESSION

M. *Maintaining the Integrity of the Profession.* The social worker should uphold and advance the values, ethics, knowledge, and mission of the profession.

N. *Community Service.* The social worker should assist the profession in making social services available to the general public.

O. *Development of Knowledge.* The social worker should take responsibility for identifying, developing, and fully utilizing knowledge for professional practice.

VI. THE SOCIAL WORKER'S ETHICAL RESPONSIBILITY TO SOCIETY

P. *Promoting the General Welfare.* The social worker should promote the general welfare of society.

2. National Association of Black Social Workers

In America today, no Black person, except the selfish or irrational, can claim neutrality in the quest for Black liberation nor fail to consider the implications of the events taking place in our society. Given the necessity for committing ourselves to the struggle for freedom, we as Black Americans practicing in the field of social welfare set forth this statement of ideals and guiding principles.

If a sense of community awareness is a precondition to humanitarian acts, then we as Black social workers must use our knowledge of the Black Community, our commitments to its self-determination and our helping skills for the benefit of Black people as we marshal our expertise to improve the quality of life of Black people. Our activities will be guided by our Black consciousness, our determination to pro-

This Code of Ethics is reprinted with the permission of the National Association of Black Social Workers.

tect the security of the Black community and to serve as advocates to relieve suffering of Black people by any means necessary.

Therefore, as Black social workers we commit ourselves, collectively, to the interests of our Black brethren and as individuals subscribe to the following statements:

I regard as my primary obligation the welfare of the Black individual, Black family and Black community and will engage in action for improving social conditions.

I give precedence to this mission over my personal interests.

I adopt the concept of a Black extended family and embrace all Black people as my brothers and sisters, making no distinction between their destiny and my own.

I hold myself responsible for the quality and extent of service I perform and the quality and extent of service performed by the agency or organization in which I am employed, as it relates to the Black Community.

I accept the responsibility to protect the Black community against unethical and hypocritical practice by any individuals or organizations engaged in social welfare activities.

I stand ready to supplement my paid or professional advocacy with voluntary service in the Black public interest.

I will consciously use my skills, and my whole being, as an instrument for social change, with particular attention directed to the establishment of Black social institutions.

3. International Federation of Social Workers

Social work originates variously from humanitarian, religious and democratic ideals and philosophies and has universal application to meet human needs arising from personal-societal interactions and to develop human potential. Professional Social Workers are dedicated to serv-

---

This Code of Ethics was adopted by the International Federation of Social Workers General Meeting, San Juan, Puerto Rico, July 10, 1976, reprinted with the permission of the International Federation of Social Workers.

ice for the welfare and self-fulfillment of human beings; to the development and disciplined use of scientific knowledge regarding human and societal behaviour; to the development of resources to meet individual, group, national and international needs and aspirations; and to the achievement of social justice.

Principles

1. Every human being has a unique value, irrespective of origin, ethnicity, sex, age, beliefs, social and economic status or contribution to society.
2. Each individual has the right of self-fulfillment to the degree that it does not encroach upon the same right of others.
3. Each society, regardless of its form, should function to provide the maximum benefits for all of its members.
4. The professional Social Worker has the responsibility to devote objective and disciplined knowledge and skill to aid individuals, groups, communities, and societies in their development and resolution of personal-societal conflicts and their consequences.
5. The professional Social Worker has a primary obligation to the objective of service, which must take precedence over self-interest aims or views.

Standards of Ethical Conduct
General

1. Seek and understand the worth of each individual and the elements which condition behaviour and the service required.
2. Uphold and advance the values, knowledge and methodology of the profession, refraining from any behavior which damages the functioning of the profession.
3. Clarify all public statements or actions whether on an individual basis or as a representative of a professional association, agency or organization.
4. Recognize professional and personal limitations, encourage the utilization of all relevant knowledge and skills and apply scientific methods of inquiry.

5. Contribute professional expertise to the development of sound policies and programs to better the quality of life in each society.
6. Identify and interpret the social needs, the basis and nature of individual, group, community, national and international social problems, and the work of the social work profession.

Relative to Clients

1. Maintain the client's right to a relationship of mutual trust, to privacy and confidentiality, and to responsible use of information. The collection and sharing of information or data shall only be related to the professional service function to be performed with the client informed as to its necessity and use. No information shall be released without prior knowledge and informed consent of the client, except where the client cannot be responsible or others may be seriously jeopardized.
2. Recognize and respect the individual goals, responsibilities, and differences of clients. Within the scope of the agency and the clients social milieu, the professional service shall assist clients to take responsibility for personal actions and to help all clients with equal willingness. Where the professional service cannot be provided under such conditions the client shall be so informed in such a way as to leave the client free to act.
3. Help the client—individual, group, community, or society—to achieve self-fulfillment and maximum potential within the limits of the equal rights of others. The service shall be based upon helping the client to understand and use the professional relationship, in furtherance of the clients legitimate desires and interests.

Relative to Agencies & Organizations

1. Work or cooperate with those agencies and organizations whose policies, procedures, and operations are directed toward adequate service delivery and encouragement of professional practice consistent with the Code of Ethics.
2. Responsibly execute the stated aims and functions of the agency or organization,

contributing to the development of sound policies, procedures, and practice in order to obtain the best possible standards of service.

3. Sustain ultimate responsibility to the client, initiating desirable alterations of policy, procedures, and practice through appropriate agency and organizational channels. If necessary remedies are not achieved after channels have been exhausted, initiate appropriate appeals to higher authorities or the wider community of interest.

4. Insure professional accountability to client and community for efficiency and effectiveness through periodic review of client, agency and organizational problems and self-performance.

Relative to Colleagues

1. Respect the training and performance of colleagues and other professionals extending all necessary cooperation that will enhance effective services.

2. Respect differences of opinion and practice of colleagues and other professionals, expressing criticism through appropriate channels in a responsible manner.

3. Promote and share opportunities for knowledge, experience, and ideas with all professional colleagues, other professionals and volunteers for the purpose of mutual improvement and validation.

4. Bring any violations of client interest or professional ethics and standards to the attention of the appropriate bodies and defend colleagues against unjust actions.

Relative to the Profession

1. Maintain the values, knowledge and methodology of the profession and contribute to their clarification and improvement.

2. Uphold the professional standards of practice and work for their advancement.

3. Defend the profession against unjust criticism and work to increase confidence in the necessity for professional practice.

4. Encourage new approaches and methodologies needed to meet new and existing needs.

Appendix C

SUMMARY OF NASW PROCEDURES FOR RECEIVING COMPLAINTS AGAINST MEMBERS FOR ALLEGED UNETHICAL CONDUCT*

Procedures for handling complaints against members who allegedly engage in unethical conduct have been established by the NASW in order to protect the public against such unethical conduct, to discipline members whose behavior has been found to be in violation of the code of ethics, and at the same time to protect members from irresponsible accusations of unethical conduct.

The adjudication procedures are not formal legal hearings and, therefore, do not observe many legal strictures and formalities. Using far greater discretion and latitude than a court, the committee of inquiry, composed of fellow NASW members, attempts to weigh the charges and reach an objective determination on the basis of the evidence and testimony presented before it. Here we will review only the first and last steps of the adjudication process, that is, the filing of the complaint and the sanctions available to the committee in case of finding the complaint justified.

I. *The Complaint*

1. Any person may file a complaint alleging unethical conduct by a social worker, but the person who allegedly violated the code of ethics must be an NASW member.

2. The complaint must be filed on an official form with the local

---

* This summary is based on the NASW Procedures, approved by the Board of Directors, October 6, 1970, and revised June 22, 1972, and June 15, 1978. At this writing further revisions are contemplated.

NASW chapter. If the person against whom the complaint is filed is not a member of a specific NASW chapter, but a member-at-large, the complaint shall be filed with the national office.

3. The complaint must charge the violation of a specific paragraph of the Code of Ethics.

4. The alleged unethical behavior must have occurred (or come to the complainant's attention) no more than sixty days before the complaint is filed.

5. The complainant must have personal knowledge about the alleged behavior and must be able and willing to provide relevant and reliable testimony to the commission on inquiry.

6. The complainant must agree to keep the adjudication procedures confidential.

The complaint must meet *all* of the above criteria before it will be accepted for adjudication.

II. *Sanctions*

If the committee of inquiry, after weighing the evidence and testimony, finds that the complaint was justified and that the NASW member did engage in unethical behavior, it shall state its findings in a written report and make recommendations for sanctions to the chapter executive committee. The chapter executive committee may approve the report or remand it to the committee for further study. Among the sanctions available for recommendation are:

1. Compensation by the respondent to the person(s) harmed by the unethical conduct.

2. Censure by the chapter or by the National Board of Directors.

3. Suspension or permanent exclusion from NASW and/or ACSW membership.

4. Publication of findings and sanctions imposed.

5. Referral to state licensing authority for further disciplinary action.

The complainant and the respondent shall have the right to appeal the chapter's decision within thirty days. If neither appeals, the recommendations will be implemented by the chapter, except that sanctions involving membership and publication of findings require the approval of the National Board of Directors.

Index

Index of Exemplars

(Text exemplars are listed by page; exemplars from Appendix A, pp. 99–103, by letter designation.)

Ethical Decisions was typeset at Five Star Typographers, Neenah, Wisconsin, printed and bound by Kingsport Press, Kingsport, Tennessee. Cover design was by Charles Kling and Associates. Internal design was by F. E. Peacock Publishers, Inc., art department. The typeface is Times Roman with Universal Bold display type.